CW00853704

Murray McBride was born in London and grew up outside the Christian faith, but life changed when he encountered God while farming in Devon. Murray met his future wife Karin when they were both serving in the Lee Abbey community in 1982. He began to learn to communicate the Christian faith to young people as a full-time youth worker in Torquay. He trained as an evangelist with the Church of England's Church Army and, for over ten years, led national missions and supported local churches in their outreach to the community. Recognized for his use of creative evangelism, Murray was presented with the Cuthbert Bardsley award. He has written several evangelistic leaflets and is the a book, *Lifesavers*. Resp........g to God's call, he trained further at Trinity Theological College Bristol and is now an ordained minister in the Anglican Church. Working with several parishes first in the diocese of Lincoln and then in Carlisle, he continues to seek new and enjoyable ways of training others to discover a living faith of their own. Murray drives a 30-year-old MG sports car and is passionate about chocolate. He enjoys walking in the Cumbrian mountains with Karin, watching movies and using creative means to share the life-changing message of Jesus with colour, joy and imagination.

## Important Information

### Photocopying permission

### The Copyright Licensing Agency (CLA)

*BRF is a Registered Charity (No. 233280)*

**Published by**
**The Bible Reading Fellowship**
First Floor, Elsfield Hall
15–17 Elsfield Way, Oxford OX2 8FG
Website: www.brf.org.uk

ISBN 1 84101 360 9
First published 2005
10  9  8  7  6  5  4  3  2  1  0

**Acknowledgments**
All scripture quotations are taken from the Contemporary English Version of the
Bible published by HarperCollins Publishers, copyright © 1991, 1992, 1995
American Bible Society.

A catalogue record for this book is available from the British Library

Printed in Singapore by Craft Print International Ltd

# Walking with Jesus through Advent and Christmas

## Murray McBride

An all-age 'visual pilgrimage' for the Christmas season

*This book is dedicated to Canon Peter Larkin and his wife, Molly,
for their inspiration and lifelong ministry of encouragement*

## Acknowledgments

*Special thanks for technical support and advice go to Sr Sandra Doore CA,
children's work adviser to the diocese of Lincoln, and Mrs Marilyn Small,
subject leader for religious education at Reepham Church of England primary school.*

*Thanks also to the parents and children of the parishes of Reepham, Cherry Willingham
and Fiskerton, who used the material during Advent.*

*Thanks most especially to Karin, my wife, for her words of wisdom.*

# Contents

**Walking with Jesus through Advent and Christmas: The visual pilgrimage**

# Foreword

I first became aware of the manuscript of *Walking with Jesus through Advent and Christmas* when visiting Murrie McBride while working in the Lincoln Diocese. I walked into the study to find sheets of paper stuck to the walls and also over the floor. The project seemed dynamic and visionary and immediately grabbed my attention and desire to know more. The pictures joined up to form a frieze journey of people from both the Old and New Testaments, taking us from creation to Mary and Joseph's escape to Egypt. The journey seemed seamless and, for the first time, made sense as a whole story.

The thing that struck me most with this project was its flexibility. I quickly became aware of the possibilities of using the material with children, adults, or children and adults together. The setting could be within the home, in the church, or in the school environment. There were short and long journeys and the daily content was neither too short nor too long.

There were endless opportunities for discussion and colouring in the pictures. I found the drawings irresistible and wanted to start colouring straight away. The pictures were ideal for younger members of the group to fill in, while the older members could read the Bible reading and journey guide and lead the prayer for the day.

The pictures of the journey could be mounted on to the wall as a frieze or kept in a folder to be flicked through. Children and adults could see how the Bible fitted together as a whole as well as being full of individual life stories of ordinary people.

This book is a real alternative to the secularized Advent calendar and will help families to study God's word together as a unit.

In the schools context, this book can aid the study of Christmas in a new and exciting way, giving teachers new material to work with that is fun, but thought-provoking at the same time. Some of the pictures could be enlarged to A2 size and used during year assembly times.

I see this book as a complete all-rounder and a must for every home and school. Rarely can you find material that is different and visionary, but with this book I feel that I have found something that I can use annually for years to come.

*Sandra Doore CA, Diocesan Development Officer for Children's Work, Diocese of Newcastle*

# The Christmas Maporama

However you plan to use the material in this book, before you start your Advent journey put the 'big picture' together to see the possible routes the travellers took on that first Christmas journey.

## Assembling the Maporama

Photocopy pages 8–19 on to A4 paper. Each section of the map is identified with a letter (A–L).

Join Section A to Section B; then join Section C to the bottom edge of Section A, and Section D to the bottom edge of Section B. Continue to follow this pattern as per the illustration. Finally, join the top ten sections together in a pattern of two columns and five rows as shown. The final two sections (K and L) are joined separately to show a small-scale map of the area.

| | |
|---|---|
| Section A | Section B |
| Section C | Section D |
| Section E | Section F |
| Section G | Section H |
| Section I | Section J |
| Section K | Section L |

Section **A** adjoins section **B**
Section **C** adjoins section **D**
Section **E** adjoins section **F**
Section **G** adjoins section **H**
Section **I** adjoins section **J**
Section **K** adjoins section **L**

The key shows the possible routes the travellers took, as follows:

→   Mary's journey to Elizabeth

↻   The wise men's journey to Bethlehem

▢▢   Joseph and Mary's journey to Bethlehem

·····   The shepherds' journey to Bethlehem

▷   The wise men's escape route home

❯   Joseph, Mary and Jesus' escape route to Egypt

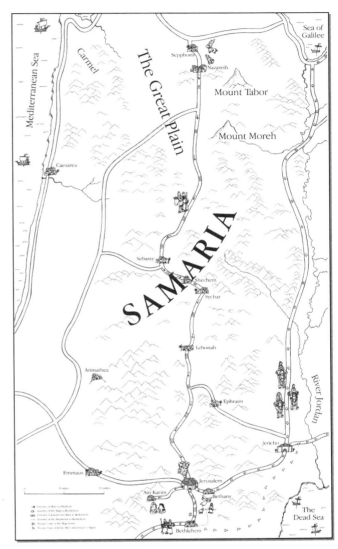

7

The Great

Carmel

Mediterranean Sea

Reproduced with permission from *Walking with Jesus through Advent and Christmas* published by BRF 2005 (1 84101 360 9) www.barnabasinchurches.org.uk

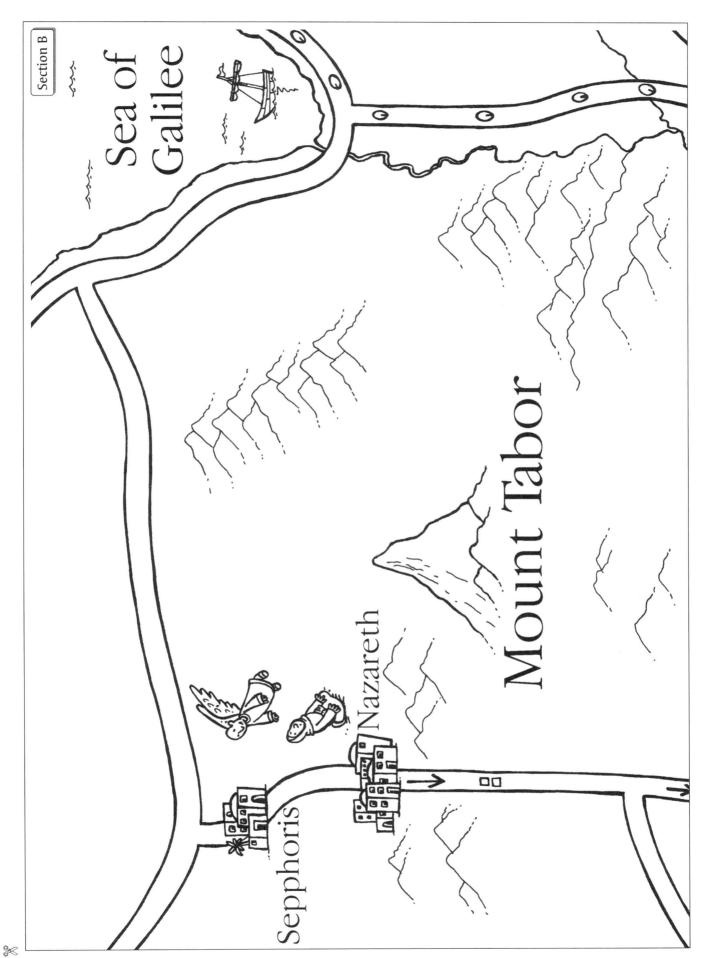

Sea of Galilee

Mount Tabor

Nazareth

Sepphoris

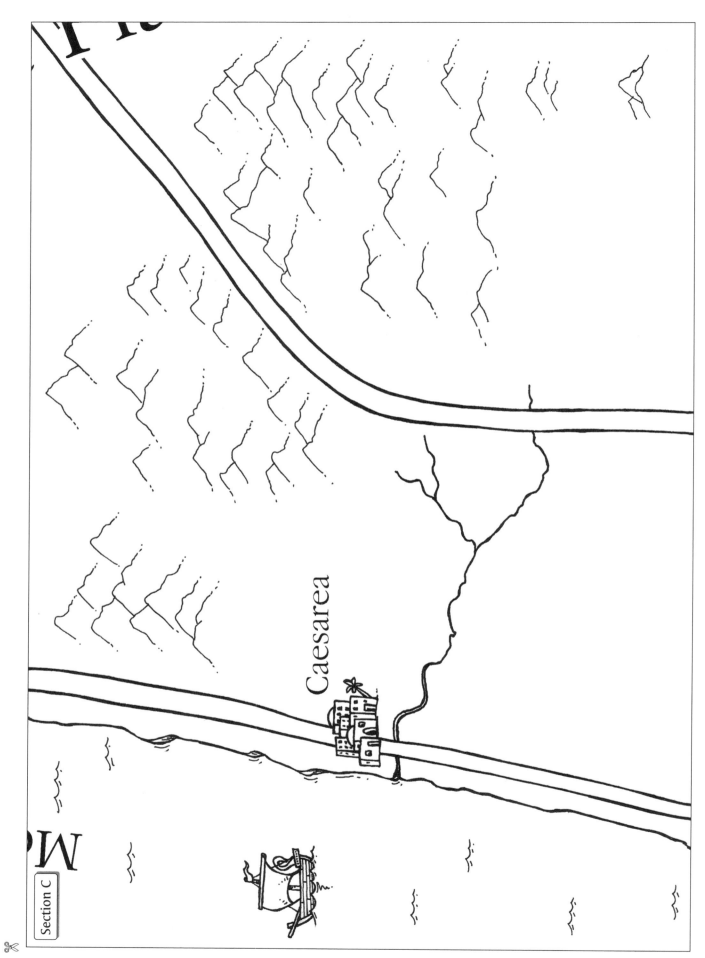

Caesarea

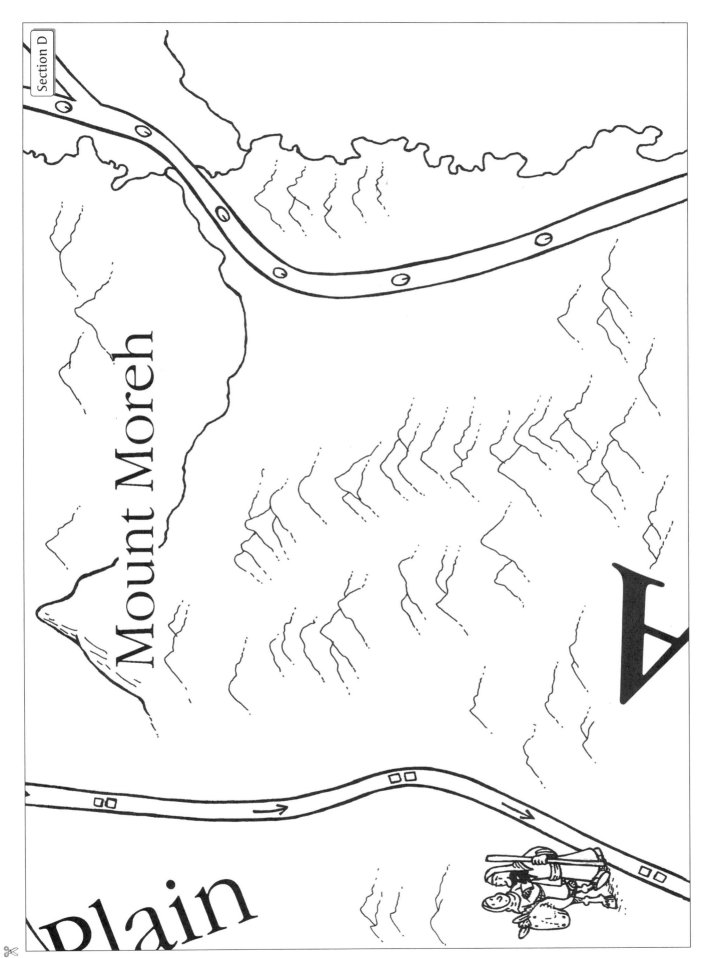

Mount Moreh

plain

Sebaste

Reproduced with permission from *Walking with Jesus through Advent and Christmas* published by BRF 2005 (1 84101 360 9) www.barnabasinchurches.org.uk

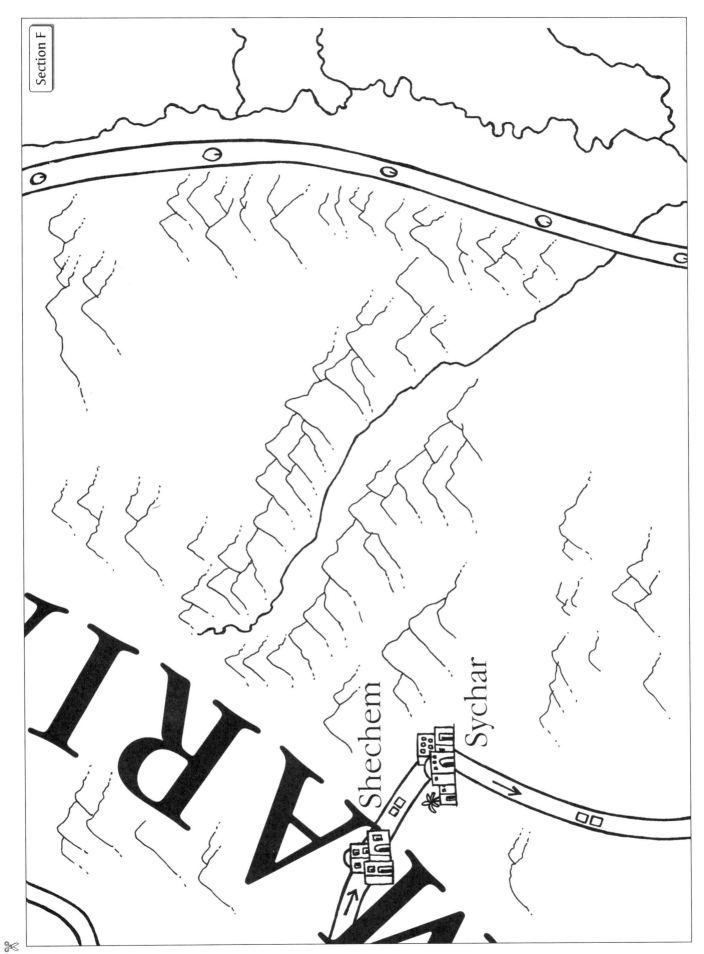

Shechem

Sychar

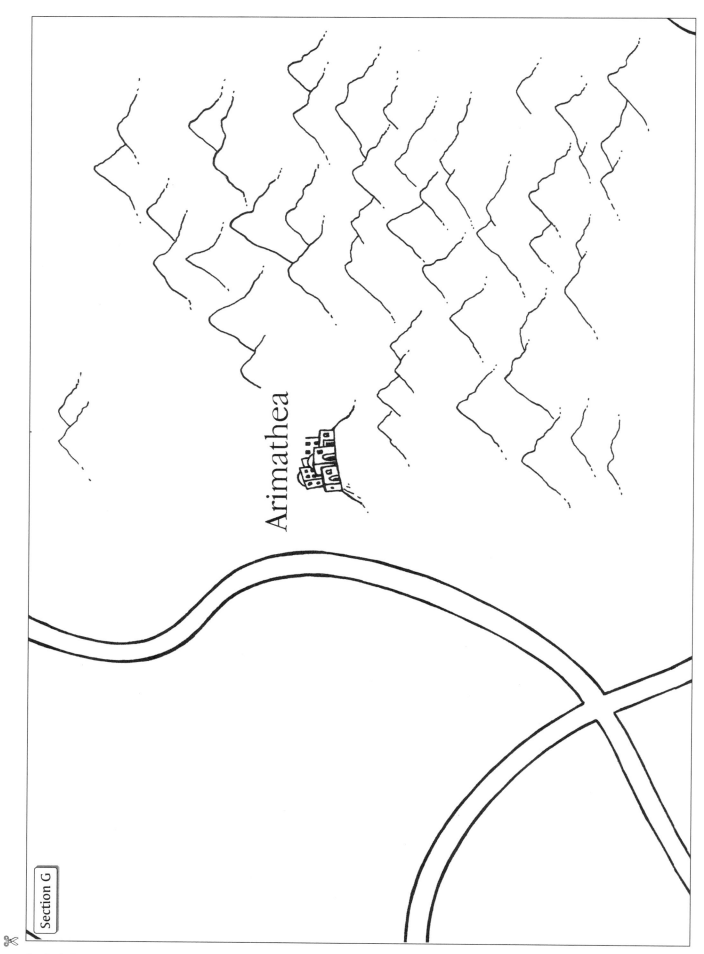

Arimathea

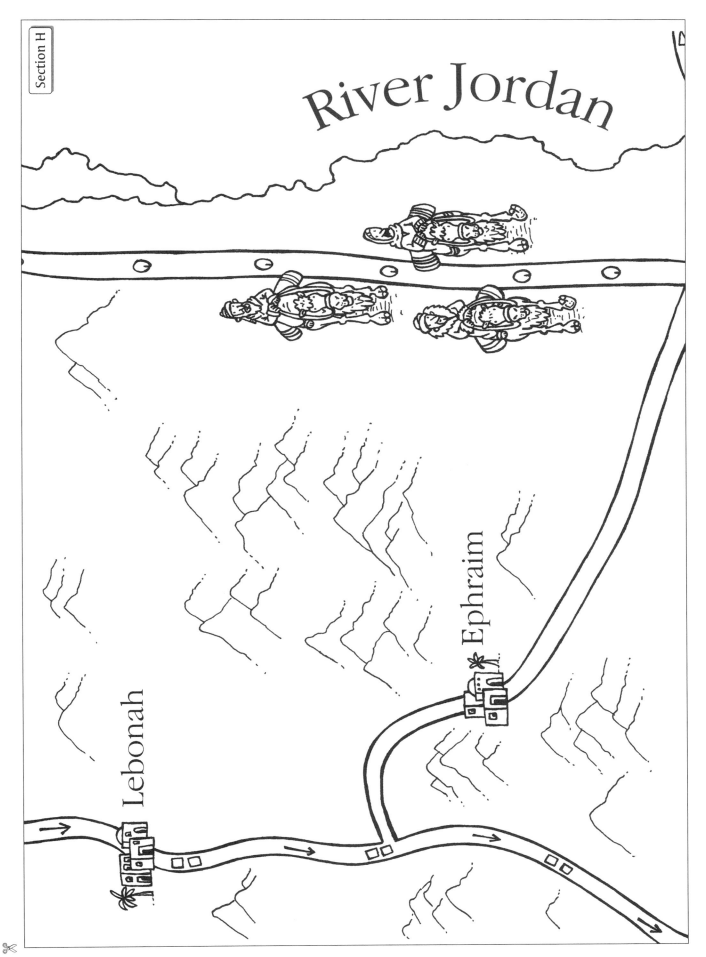

River Jordan

Ephraim

Lebonah

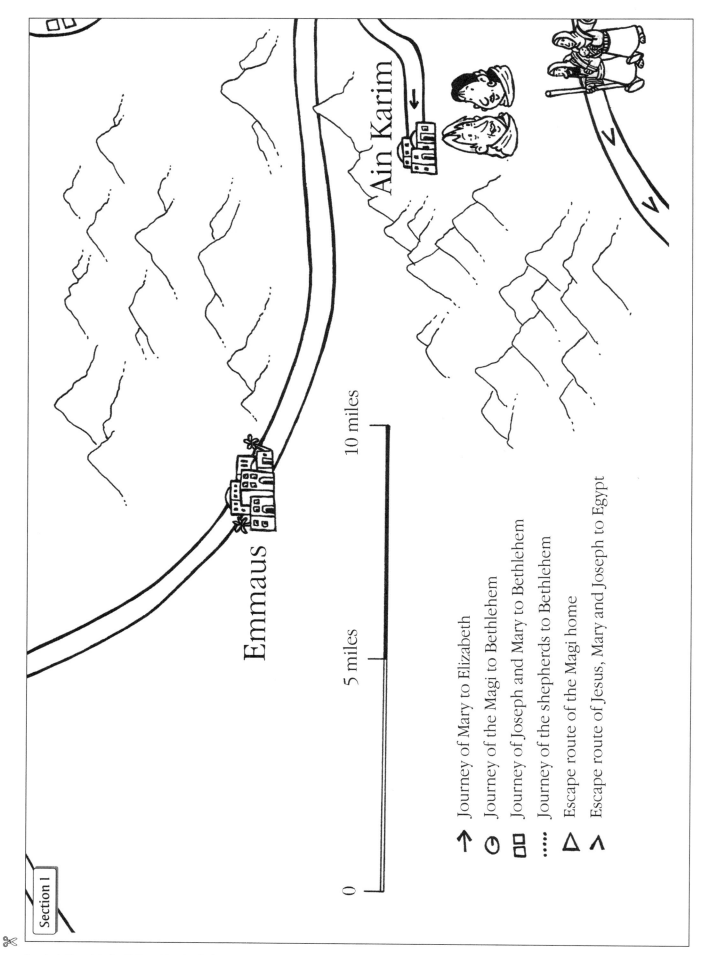

Ain Karim

Emmaus

0          5 miles          10 miles

↑  Journey of Mary to Elizabeth
⊙  Journey of the Magi to Bethlehem
⊡  Journey of Joseph and Mary to Bethlehem
⋮  Journey of the shepherds to Bethlehem
△  Escape route of the Magi home
∨  Escape route of Jesus, Mary and Joseph to Egypt

Section 1

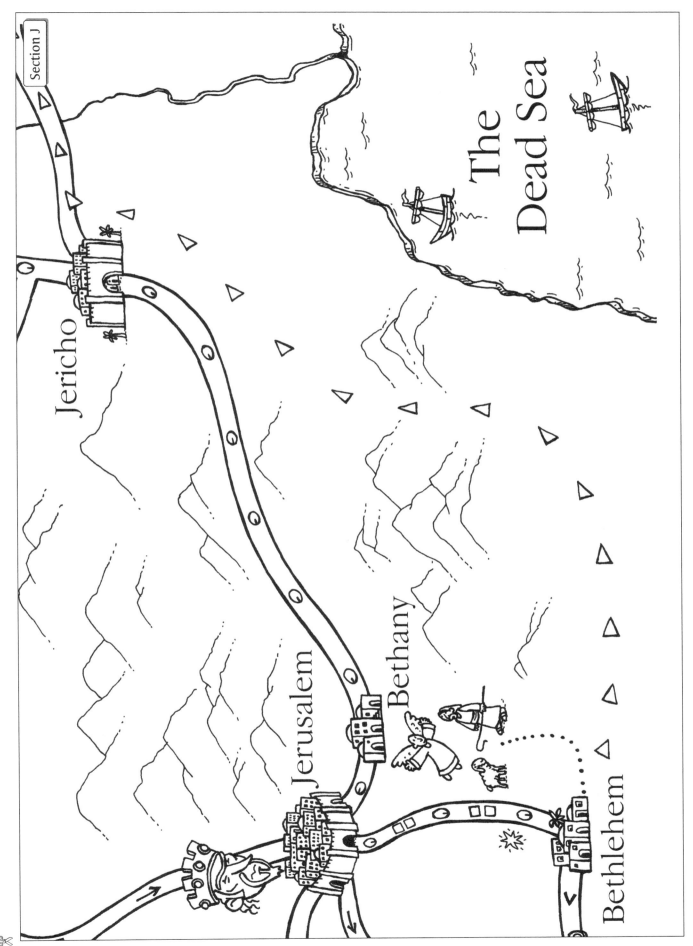

The Dead Sea

Jericho

Jerusalem

Bethany

Bethlehem

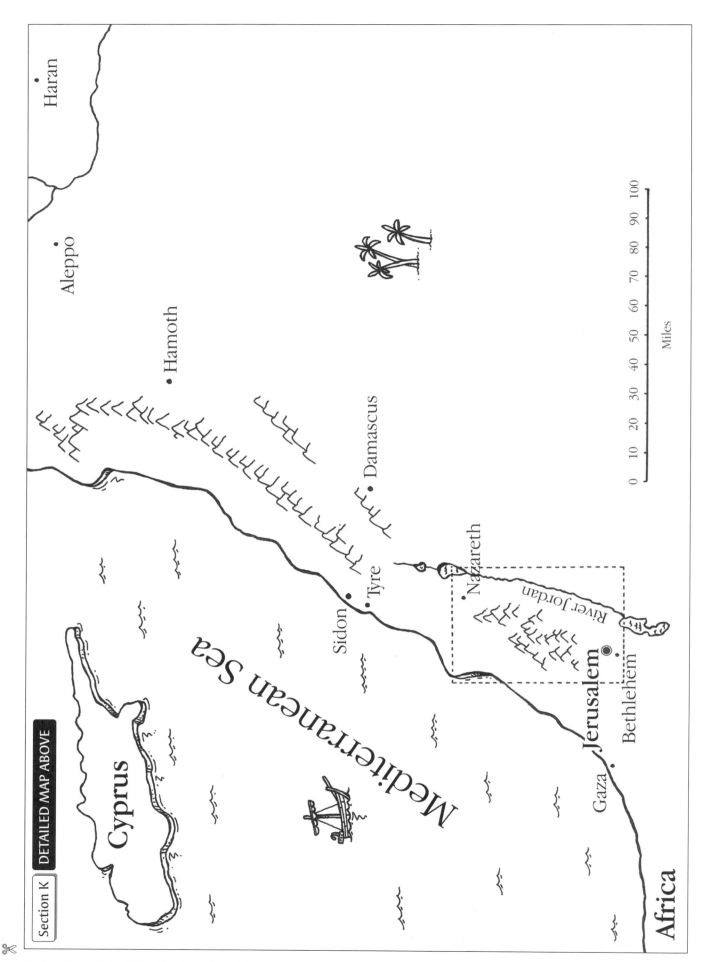

Section K

DETAILED MAP ABOVE

Haran

Aleppo

Hamoth

Damascus

Tyre

Sidon

Nazareth

River Jordan

Jerusalem

Bethlehem

Gaza

Cyprus

Mediterranean Sea

Africa

0  10  20  30  40  50  60  70  80  90  100

Miles

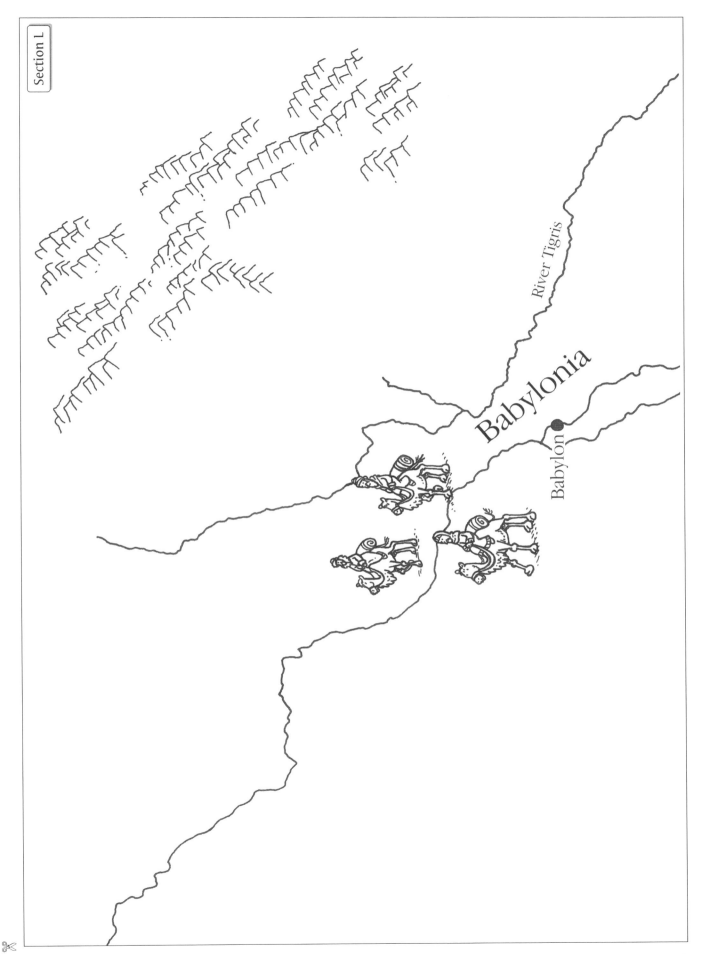

River Tigris

Babylonia

● Babylon

# Introduction

The *Advent*ure of Christmas begins: prepare for the life-changing experience of celebrating Christmas! This resource is designed for use by people of all ages as a creative way for the whole family, individuals, church-based groups or schools to prepare for Christmas. This 'visual pilgrimage' for Advent presents the story of Christmas by examining in detail the biblical events set out in the Gospels of Matthew and Luke.

Because God's Christmas message is so awe-inspiring a thought, so wonderful an invitation and such a challenge to our daily lives, Christians have traditionally used the four weeks leading up to Christmas—the season of Advent—as a period in which to prepare. During this time, people plan to take time each day to pray and read the Bible. This resource is designed to help groups of all ages and any size to plan time to walk with Jesus in the busy lead-up to Christmas. You are prayerfully invited to come on a spiritual journey, to pause, stand in the shoes of biblical characters who made the original journey, and reflect on the important choices they made. *Walking with Jesus through Advent and Christmas* is a biblical story-map, designed to guide you through the Christmas narratives, either as a daily devotion or a weekly project, depending on your need.

### A panoramic view of the Christmas narrative

The material retells the biblical events in a visual form to enable us to follow with our own eyes and imagination in the footsteps of the people who played a part in the very first Christmas, starting as far back as Adam and moving right the way through to the escape to Egypt after Jesus was born. In this way, the material endeavours to include the interesting, the dramatic and even the obscure parts of Christmas, so often forgotten or neglected.

### An interactive resource for study and worship

The material has been devised in order to help people of all ages to engage mentally, spiritually and creatively with the story of Christmas. Each step of the story is intended to be a spiritual exercise for the imagination. The provision of a colouring activity is offered to facilitate a deeper engagement with God, as colour and texture, light and darkness give shape to the reality of the first Christmas and our own spiritual journey.

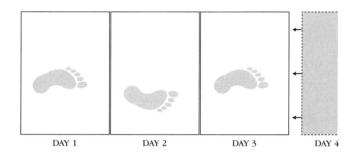

DAY 1    DAY 2    DAY 3    DAY 4

## How to use the material

Each daily step of the story-map is designed to be photocopied so that each person using the material has their own copy to colour and reflect on. The steps are then joined together to create a truly scriptural Advent frieze with a complete overview of the Christmas story, from the first steps of Adam to the baby steps of Jesus.

However, this is more than a biblical frieze; it is a teaching tool to help adults and children alike see the great sweep of God's work present in the story of Christmas. Sadly, it is all too easy for us to get a bit disjointed or lost as we turn the pages of the Bible, forgetting what went before and after. *Walking with Jesus through Advent and Christmas* helps us to join up the story, giving the complete message of Christmas in one unified and memorable presentation.

# Using the material in the family

## Plan time together

Plan to have a special time together every day to work on the activities. Help your children by investing time with them.

## Use your imagination

Look at the daily footprint icons together. Discuss together whose footsteps are in the picture, think about what the visual clues around the footprints say about how the characters fit into the story of Christmas, and see how the followers of God move in the same direction.

## Use the resource as a menu

Think of the daily reflections as a menu. You don't always have to use all the material. If you have a child who can read, you may choose to use the mini-map material with them (see pages 30–31), inviting them to read the story themselves, or reading to them while they colour in the story-map page.

## Build up the biggest Advent calendar ever!

The heart of the experience is to build up the Christmas story-map and follow the footsteps of all the people involved in the original journey. Each day, after the relevant part of the story-map has been coloured in, attach it to the previous parts so that the whole Christmas story slowly comes together in a long Advent frieze to hang on the wall or unfold on the floor.

## Walk with Jesus through Advent and Christmas

Start from the beginning of the story-map each day and retrace your steps, recalling the story so far. Each step of the story-map has a number and key Bible verse to help identify each part of the story as it unfolds. As the frieze gets longer, you don't need to concentrate on every single step; rather, pick out those that have been of particular significance for you. Discuss together whose footsteps they are, read the short Bible verse beneath the icon, and reflect on that part of the journey.

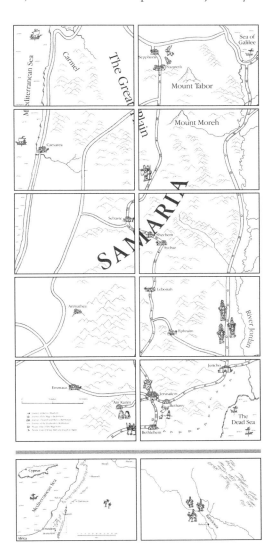

## Use the Maporama

Pages 8–19 contain the component parts of a big map, which we have called a 'Maporama', giving you a bird's-eye panoramic view of the many journeys described in the Bible, leading to the birth of Christ. Photocopy each page of the Maporama and put it together to act as an ongoing visual aid. Keep it handy as a means to help you appreciate the adventures and dangers that people encountered on the first Christmas journey.

# Using the material with adults

## Plan to make time in your day

Advent is a season of Christian discipline, so challenge yourself to put aside time to walk with God every day. This is not intended to be a sacrifice, but an oasis—an investment in your spiritual life and an opportunity to gain a deeper understanding of Christmas.

## Develop your spiritual imagination

Sadly, as we get older, most of us overlook the gift of imagination to develop our faith. Yet this is one of the most powerful forces we have to influence and motivate us. Study the footprint icon for the day. Each one was created prayerfully to express the scripture reading and link into the great *Advent*ure of God who came to live among us. Reflect on the picture with eyes of faith and put yourself in that person's shoes. The purpose of the footprint icon is to help us to link up each part of the Christmas story into one epic adventure of God's salvation through Christ.

## Use the resource as a menu

Think of the daily reflections as a menu. If you have time and are hungry to know more, feel free to use all the material. However, sometimes 'less is more' and on those days just take what you need from the menu. Advent reminds us that developing our faith in Christ is about quality, not quantity.

## Build the Christmas story

The heart of the experience is literally to put together the Christmas story. The material pieces together the original accounts in Luke and Matthew to recreate the whole story from the Gospel fragments.

Follow in the footsteps of the different characters involved in the first Christmas. Join each day's picture to the preceding day's and see the biblical narrative grow as you join the footsteps together. Creating a story-map of the Christmas story produces an Advent frieze to hang on the wall or unfold on the floor.

## Be creative: express your spirituality in colour

This resource is designed to enable you to engage with the Bible in a visual and imaginative way. As you colour the daily footsteps icon, express your understanding of the scriptures and reflect on the dilemmas, dramas and emotions of everyday life in a colour scheme of your own. Use colour to express yourself spiritually.

## Use the Maporama

Pages 8–19 contain the component parts of a big map, which we have called a 'Maporama', giving you a bird's-eye panoramic view of the many journeys described in the Bible, leading to the birth of Christ. Photocopy each page of the Maporama and put it together to act as an ongoing visual aid. Keep it handy as a means to help you appreciate the adventures and dangers that people encountered on the first Christmas journey.

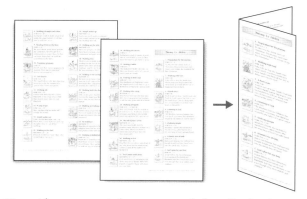

## Use the material as a tool for faith-sharing

Advent can be a great opportunity for faith-sharing. Once the map is complete, it can be used as an attractive method of explaining the message of Christmas to enquiring adults, simply by walking with Jesus each day and building up the Christmas story. On pages 32–33 you will find 'mini-maps' to help you explain the whole message to an adult.

# Using the material with children

## Plan your time carefully

Read through all the session material to gain an overview of the resource and help you decide how you will use it. You may plan to:

★ Use the material day-by-day from the beginning of Advent, through Christmas and into Epiphany.
★ Divide the material into four parts, covering approximately seven days' worth in each weekly session (four sessions in total).
★ Hold an activity day to work through all the material in a single session.

## Use your imagination

Introduce the idea of footsteps to the group. Invite the children to draw around their feet, cut out the foot shapes and create a trail of footprints on a long roll of paper (lining wallpaper is ideal for this). Invite the children to follow the trail by walking in each footprint. Then explain that we are going to imagine we are walking in the footsteps of the people who went on the first Christmas journey to Bethlehem.

## Use the resource as a menu

Because the material has been written for use in a number of ways, in a group situation there will probably be more material than you will have time to explore. Think of the daily reflections as a menu of options in which the key resources will be the Bible verse and the 'journey guide' explaining the storyline. The suggestions given for colouring in will help to give the children ideas.

## Colour in and build up the Christmas story-map

The heart of the experience is literally to put together the Christmas story and follow in the footsteps of the different characters involved in the first Christmas. Each of the different steps could be given to a different person to colour in. Invite them to look and think about their own piece of the journey and choose colours that are best suited to their part of the story.

## Putting the whole Christmas Adventure together

Building up the story-map is an important part of the learning process, so start joining the footsteps together as soon as you can. Each step of the story-map has a number and key Bible verse to help identify each part of the story as it unfolds. Depending on your timescale, at the end of a single day, or after several days or weeks, you will have built up the whole Christmas story in a long Advent frieze, which can be either hung on the wall or unfolded on the floor. The finished frieze is approximately ten metres long.

## Use the Maporama

Pages 8–19 contain the component parts of a big map, which we have called a 'Maporama', giving you and your group a bird's-eye panoramic view of the many journeys described in the Bible, leading to the birth of Christ. Photocopy each page of the Maporama and put it together to act as an ongoing visual aid. Keep it handy as a means to help you appreciate the adventures and dangers that people encountered on the first Christmas journey.

# Four ready-to-use sessions for use with children

## Notes for teachers

The *Walking with Jesus* material was originally designed as an Advent journey with daily notes for a family or individual. The same format is not always suitable for groups, so, to make the experience accessible to schools or church-based groups, the same material has been divided up into four group sessions, with ready-to-use class work for teachers. If appropriate, the four sessions can follow the four weeks of Advent.

### Dividing up the work so that everyone can participate

There are 31 pictures in total in the story-map frieze. Dividing this into four weeks' worth of material means that there are seven to eight pictures in each session. With smaller groups, this means that children can work on the pictures singly or in twos or threes. With larger groups, you will need to have seven or eight people in each group. Dividing the material in this way gives the added benefit of seeing how the different groups interpret the story through the use of colour and texture, light and darkness.

### Using mini-maps for bite-sized teaching

If you do not have time to use the full teaching notes, on pages 30–31 you will find mini-maps to use with your class or group. Mini-maps comprise a simple summary of the teaching notes, giving a bite-sized explanation of each part of the Christmas journey found in the story-map.

---

### SESSION ONE

## The journey of Christmas begins

 *Pictures 1–8*

*Session time: 30 minutes*

### Contents

1. Preparation for the journey (Luke 1:1, 3–4)
2. Walking with God (Luke 3:38)
3. A fresh start (Luke 3:36)
4. Listening to God (Luke 3:34)
5. Ordinary people (Luke 3:31–32)
6. A family tree of faith (Luke 3:23–24)
7. God's plan for our lives (Luke 1:5–7)
8. Walking through God's plan (Luke 1:8–20)

### Preparation

Read the session notes below and prepare to have fun!

**You will need:**
★ Felt-tipped pens, crayons or paints (bear in mind that paints take more time to clear up)
★ A roll of sticky tape to join the children's work together (if using paints, allow the pictures to dry before joining them together)
★ Photocopies of the eight pictures (enough for each child in each group)
★ A few large sheets of paper or card to make the illustrated footprints for the footprint exercise (optional)

## Introduction

Share the idea with the children that we can follow the footprints left by people who have gone before us. We can see the mark left by people's shoes on soft earth, on snow, on sand or in the trail left by wet shoes on a wooden or stone floor. We can follow a person we cannot see, who may have left those footprints minutes, hours, days or even weeks ago.

As we read the Christmas story, it's like following in the tracks of the people who took part in the first Christmas—marks left years ago, but preserved in the pages of the Bible for us to follow.

## Making tracks (an optional footprint exercise)

We all make some marks as we walk. If you look carefully, you can tell the difference between one person's shoe tracks or footprints and another's. This is part of the skill of tracking.

Put a little water (1cm deep) in a shallow bowl. Carefully put a foot or sole of a shoe in the water, then immediately make a footprint or track on some paper. Draw around the water print before it dries out. Now you can see your unique footprint or track and follow your trail.

## The journey of Christmas begins

Divide the children into eight groups of roughly equal size. Each group will work with one of the eight pictures. You will need to give each child a copy of the picture allocated to his or her group. Read the story from the children's mini-maps for pictures 1–8 while the children study their picture.

## Colouring the story

Encourage the children to think about the part of the Christmas story they have been given and then to choose carefully the colours they want to use before starting their work. Allow them time to colour or paint their picture.

## Walking through the story

When all the pictures have been coloured, you will need to choose one from each of the eight groups to be joined together to create a large frieze. The sections are all numbered for ease of identification. Put the frieze up on the wall or unfold it along the floor, and invite each group to walk through this first part of the Christmas journey (perhaps asking why people used different shading or colours or added something to the picture).

## Time of prayer or reflection

The Bible explains that talking and listening to God is called prayer. Encourage the children to talk to God as the prayer below is prayed, or, if they prefer, invite them to use the time to think about the first steps they have taken on the journey to Christmas. Explain that when we say 'Amen' at the end of the prayer, this means 'Let it be so' or 'I agree'.

 Great God of all time and history, thank you that none of us is so small that you forget us. Help us to see the importance of the part we play in our world. This Christmas, may we see you more clearly, love you more dearly and follow you more nearly day by day. Amen

### SESSION TWO:

# The story of God's special baby

 *Pictures 9–16*

 *Session time: 30 minutes*

### Contents

9. Reading between the lines (John 21:25)
10. Promises, promises (Luke 2:5)
11. God-bearer (Luke 1:26–38)
12. Walking tall (Luke 1:39–45)
13. A song of joy (Luke 1:46–55)
14. Joseph walks out (Luke 1:56 and Matthew 1:18–19)
15. Walking in the dark (Matthew 1:20–23)
16. Joseph wakes up (Matthew 1:24)

### Preparation

Read the session notes below and prepare to have fun!

**You will need:**
★ Felt-tipped pens, crayons or paints (bear in mind that paints take more time to clear up)
★ A roll of sticky tape to join the children's work together (if using paints, allow the pictures to dry before joining them together)
★ Photocopies of the eight pictures (enough for each child in each group)
★ Footprints from the footprint exercise in Session One (optional)

## Introduction

Remind the children that we can follow the footprints left by people who have gone before us. We can see the mark left by people's shoes on soft earth, on snow, on sand or in the trail left by wet shoes on a wooden or stone floor. Can they think of any other ways to leave our footprints? We can follow a person we cannot see, who may have left those footprints minutes, hours, days or even weeks ago.

Remind them that as we read the Christmas story it's like following in the tracks of the people who took part in the first Christmas—marks left years ago, but preserved in the pages of the Bible for us to follow.

## Making tracks (an optional footprint exercise)

Talk about how we can tell the direction of a journey by looking at footprints or tracks. Encourage the children to give examples of this. Show the children one of the paper footprints from the last session. Ask the group to look carefully at the print, find the heel and toe, and think about which way the person was facing. This will tell you the direction of their journey and the direction in which you need to follow.

## The story of God's special baby

As before, divide the children into eight groups of roughly equal size. Each group will work with one of the eight pictures. Once again, you will need to give each child a copy of the picture allocated to his or her group. Read the story from the children's mini-maps for pictures 9–16 while the children study their picture.

## Colouring the story

Once again, encourage the children to think about the part of the Christmas story they have been given and then to choose carefully the colours they want to use before starting their work. Allow them time to colour or paint their picture.

## Walking through the story

Choose a picture from each group, and join the coloured sections of the frieze together in the right order. The sections are all numbered for ease of identification. Join these new sections to the frieze you made in Session One. Once again, put the frieze up on the wall or unfold it along the floor, and invite each group to walk through the Christmas journey so far (perhaps asking why people used different shading or colours or added something to the picture).

## Time of prayer or reflection

Remind the children that talking and listening to God is called prayer. Encourage them to talk to God as the prayer below is prayed, or, if they prefer, invite them to use the time to think about the steps they have taken so far on the journey to Christmas. Remind them that when we say 'Amen' at the end of the prayer, this means 'Let it be so' or 'I agree'.

 Loving God, you are like a father and mother to us. Thank you for the example of Mary and Joseph. Help us to learn to trust you more as they did, even when things go wrong. This Christmas, may we see you more clearly, love you more dearly and follow you more nearly day by day. Amen

---

### SESSION THREE:

# The story of God's plan

>  *Pictures 17–23*
>
>  *Session time: 30 minutes*

### Contents

17. Walking up the aisle (Matthew 1:25)
18. Marking time *(there is intentionally no Bible reading for this day)*
19. Walking in the starlight (Matthew 2:1)
20. Walking with the shepherds (Luke 2:8)
21. Walking and talking with God (Luke 2:36–37)
22. No walkover (Matthew 2:1)
23. Walking to Bethlehem (Luke 2:1–4)

### Preparation

Read the session notes below and prepare to have fun!

**You will need:**
★ Felt-tipped pens, crayons or paints (bear in mind that paints take more time to clear up)
★ A roll of sticky tape to join the children's work together (if using paints, allow the pictures to dry before joining them together)
★ Photocopies of the seven pictures (enough for each child in each group)
★ A few large sheets of paper or card to make the illustrated footprints for the footprint exercise (optional)

## Introduction

Once again, remind the children that we can follow the footprints left by people who have gone before us. We can see the mark left by people's shoes on soft earth, on snow, on sand or in the trail left by wet shoes on a wooden or stone floor. We can follow a person we cannot see, who may have left those footprints minutes, hours, days or even weeks ago.

As we read the Christmas story it's like following in the tracks of the people who took part in the first Christmas—marks left years ago, but preserved in the pages of the Bible for us to follow.

## Making tracks (an optional footprint exercise)

Talk about tracking. How can we tell how many people have made the tracks? When there are lots of prints, it's difficult to tell.

Select several members of the group with different shoes. As in Session One, put a little water (1cm deep) in a shallow bowl. Invite each child in turn carefully to put the soles of their shoes in the water and then immediately walk over a large sheet of paper. Mark the prints with a pen as you did in Session One. As a group, examine the footprints and try to pick out the different tracks made by each person's shoes. How easy is it to see from the prints how many people made the tracks?

## The story of God's plan

Divide the children into seven groups of roughly equal size. As before, you will need to give each child a copy of the picture allocated to his or her group. Read the story from the children's mini-maps for pictures 17–23 while the children study their picture.

## Colouring the story

As before, encourage the children to think about the part of the Christmas story they have been given and then to choose carefully the colours they want to use before starting their work. Allow them time to colour or paint their picture.

## Walking through the story

Choose a picture from each of the seven groups, and join the coloured sections of the frieze together in the right order. Join these new sections to the frieze already made. Put the frieze up on the wall or unfold it along the floor, and invite each group to walk through the Christmas journey so far (perhaps asking why people used different shading or colours or added something to the picture).

## Time of prayer or reflection

Encourage the children to talk to God as the prayer below is prayed, or, if they prefer, invite them to use the time to think about the steps they have taken so far on the journey to Christmas.

 God of all, help us to see how you were remaking our worldwide family around Jesus. This Christmas, may we see you more clearly, love you more dearly and follow you more nearly day by day. Amen

# Jesus is born

 *Pictures 24–31*

*Session time: 30 minutes*

## Contents

24. Walking the streets (Luke 2:5–7)
25. Resting a while (Luke 2:6–7)
26. A spring in their step (Luke 2:8–19)
27. Walking into a trap (Matthew 2:1–8)
28. Walking alongside (Luke 2:22–32 and 38)
29. The hill walkers arrive (Matthew 2:9–12)
30. Walking in fear (Matthew 2:16–18)
31. You'll never walk alone (Matthew 2:13–15)

## Preparation

Read the session notes below and prepare to have fun!

**You will need:**
★ Felt-tipped pens, crayons or paints (bear in mind that paints take more time to clear up)
★ A roll of sticky tape to join the children's work together (if using paints, allow the pictures to dry before joining them together)
★ Photocopies of the eight pictures (enough for each child in each group)
★ A few large sheets of paper or card to make the illustrated footprints for the footprint exercise (optional)

## Introduction

Once again, remind the children that we can follow the footprints left by people who have gone before us. We can see the mark left by people's shoes on soft earth, on snow, on sand or in the trail left by wet shoes on a wooden or stone floor. We can follow a person we cannot see, who may have left those footprints minutes, hours, days or even weeks ago.

As we read the Christmas story it's like following in the tracks of the people who took part in the first Christmas—marks left years ago, but preserved in the pages of the Bible for us to follow.

## Making tracks (an optional footprint exercise)

Start by discussing the idea that sometimes we don't want others to follow us, especially if we are being hunted by King Herod's soldiers! One way to hide our tracks is to walk backwards to make it look as if we are going in another direction. Demonstrate this to the group by using a shallow bowl of water to make wet footprints on paper as before. Ask the children to think of other ways to disguise their tracks: for example, walking up a stream (this can be dangerous!), walking on a dry hard surface, or simply changing your shoes.

## Jesus is born

Divide the children into eight groups of roughly equal size. Once again, each group will work with one of the eight pictures. You will need to give each child a copy of the picture allocated to his or her group. Read the story from the children's mini-maps for pictures 24–31 while the children study their picture.

## Colouring the story

As before, encourage the children to think about the part of the Christmas story they have been given and then carefully to choose the colours they want to use before starting their work. Allow them time to colour or paint their picture.

## Walking through the story

Choose a picture from each group and join the new sections of the frieze together in the right order (the sections are all numbered for ease of identification). Join this last part of the story to the frieze made in previous sessions. Put the completed frieze up on the wall or unfold it along the floor, and invite each group to walk through the whole Christmas journey (perhaps asking why people used different shading or colours or added something to the picture).

## Time of prayer or reflection

Encourage the children to talk to God as the prayer below is prayed, or, if they prefer, invite them to use the time to think about the final steps they have taken on the journey to Christmas.

 **All-caring God, who watches over us night and day, thank you for coming to meet us in Jesus. Help us to protect others from harm. This Christmas, may we see you more clearly, love you more dearly and follow you more nearly day by day. Amen**

# Walking with Jesus through Advent and Christmas

## The visual pilgrimage

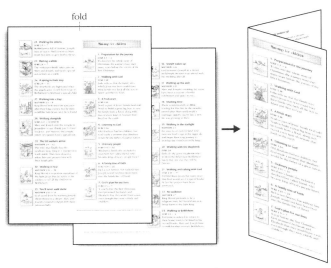

### Mini-map for children

Pages 30–31 are designed to be photocopied back to back and folded as shown to make the mini-map for teachers to use as a summary of the story-map pictures.

### Mini map for adults

Pages 32–33 are designed to be photocopied back to back and folded as shown to make the mini-map for adults to use as a faith-sharing tool for Christmas. These brief guides enable you to walk an adult through the Christmas story. The mini-map can be used as part of a presentation in church, at home or even in the street. The mini-map has been designed for use with the story-map.

### Story maps and reflections

Pages 34–95 form the visual pilgrimage for your *Walking with Jesus through Advent and Christmas* journey. The material invites you to pause a while, stand in the shoes of the biblical characters who made the original journey and consider the choices they made. For each day you will find a Bible passage to help you prepare for the journey, a journey guide giving background information as you travel, suggestions for personal reflection—one using colour to express your thoughts—and, finally, a prayer to use along the way. Each footstep has a number and key Bible verse to help identify each part of the story as it unfolds. The steps build into a Christmas story map, which can be photo-copied, coloured in and made into a long Advent frieze to hang on the wall or unroll on the floor. However, the images would work equally well as an on-the-page journey for the individual reader.

## 8. Walking through God's plan

LUKE 1:8–20

Zechariah is full of doubt when God sends the angel Gabriel to tell him that he will have a son.

## 9. Reading between the lines

JOHN 21:25

We don't know much about Joseph the carpenter, even though he is making plans to marry Mary. To find out more about him, we need to read between the lines.

## 10. Promises, promises

LUKE 2:5

Joseph and Mary were engaged to be married. They had no idea how famous they would be.

## 11. God-bearer

LUKE 1:26–38

The angel Gabriel tells Mary that God wants her to be the mother of a special baby: God's son, Jesus.

## 12. Walking tall

LUKE 1:39–45

Gabriel tells Mary that her cousin, Elizabeth, is also expecting a child. Mary travels many miles to visit Elizabeth.

## 13. A song of joy

LUKE 1:46–55

Mary declares that her baby will change the world.

## 14. Joseph walks out

LUKE 1:56 AND MATTHEW 1:18–19

When Mary tells Joseph her news, he thinks it best to call off the wedding.

## 15. Walking in the dark

MATTHEW 1:20–23

If Joseph will not marry Mary, who will believe her story?

## 16. Joseph wakes up

MATTHEW 1:24

God reassures Joseph in a dream, and Joseph decides to go ahead with the wedding after all.

## 17. Walking up the aisle

MATTHEW 1:25

Mary and Joseph's wedding day must have been a mixture of joyful celebration and quiet secrets.

## 18. Marking time

There is intentionally no Bible reading for this day. As the months passed after Mary and Joseph's marriage, quietly, day by day, a new life was growing in Mary.

## 19. Walking in the starlight

MATTHEW 2:1

Far away in an eastern land, wise men see God's sign in the night sky and begin their long journey to worship the child born to be king.

## 20. Walking with the shepherds

LUKE 2:8

Little do the poor shepherds who work in the fields near Bethlehem know that one day they will be famous.

## 21. Walking and talking with God

LUKE 2:36–37

Faithful Anna prayed for many years that God would send a special leader. At last her prayers have been answered.

## 22. No walkover

MATTHEW 2:1

King Herod pretends to be a religious man, but his real aim is to bring harm to the baby king.

## 23. Walking to Bethlehem

LUKE 2:1–4

Everyone is ordered to return to their home town to be listed in the record books. Mary and Joseph have to walk for days to reach Bethlehem.

Reproduced with permission from *Walking with Jesus through Advent and Christmas* published by BRF 2005 (1 84101 360 9) www.barnabasinchurches.org.uk

### 24. Walking the streets
LUKE 2:5–7

Bethlehem is full of visitors. Joseph tries in vain to find a room as Mary nears her time to give birth to Jesus.

### 25. Resting a while
LUKE 2:6–7

The innkeeper finally takes pity on Mary and Joseph, and God's special son is born in a stable.

### 26. A spring in their step
LUKE 2:8–19

The shepherds are frightened when the angels arrive to tell them to go to Bethlehem to find God's special child.

### 27. Walking into a trap
MATTHEW 2:1–8

King Herod welcomes the wise men after their long journey, but he plans to kill the baby Jesus once he is found.

### 28. Walking alongside
LUKE 2:22–32 AND 38

Mary and Joseph visit the temple in Jerusalem to say 'thank you' to God for Jesus, and Simeon, the temple priest, recognizes God's special son.

### 29. The hill walkers arrive
MATTHEW 2:9–12

The wise men finally find the newborn king in the town of Bethlehem. They bow down to adore him and present him with their kingly gifts.

### 30. Walking in fear
MATTHEW 2:16–18

King Herod is so jealous and afraid of the baby Jesus that he sends in his soldiers to kill all the children in Bethlehem.

### 31. You'll never walk alone
MATTHEW 2:13–15

God saves Jesus by warning Joseph about Herod in a dream. Mary and Joseph escape to Egypt with their precious baby.

## Mini-map for children

### 1. Preparation for the journey
LUKE 1:1, 3–4

To discover the whole story of Christmas, the journey must start many years before the events of the first Christmas.

### 2. Walking with God
LUKE 3:38

Luke tells us that the family into which Jesus was born could trace their family tree back all the way to Adam and then to God.

### 3. A fresh start
LUKE 3:36

Noah is part of Jesus' family. God told Noah to build a great big boat to save his family from a flood, along with two of every kind of creature that lived on the earth.

### 4. Listening to God
LUKE 3:34

Old Abraham had no children, but God made a promise that Abraham would be the father of a great nation.

### 5. Ordinary people
LUKE 3:31–32

Abraham's family also included a shepherd boy called David, who became king of God's people Israel.

### 6. A family tree of faith
LUKE 3:23–24

Heli is not famous, but without him Joseph would not have been born into the family line of David.

### 7. God's plan for our lives
LUKE 1:5–7

A year before the first Christmas, God promises Zechariah and Elizabeth that they will have a son, even though they are elderly and childless.

Reproduced with permission from *Walking with Jesus through Advent and Christmas* published by BRF 2005
(1 84101 360 9) www.barnabasinchurches.org.uk

## 9. Reading between the lines
JOHN 21:25

We don't know much about Joseph the carpenter, even though he is making plans to marry Mary. To find out more about him, we need to read between the lines.

## 10. Promises, promises
LUKE 2:5

When Mary and Joseph became engaged to be married, they had no idea of the world-changing events that would overtake them.

## 11. God-bearer
LUKE 1:26–38

The angel Gabriel tells Mary that God wants her to be the mother of a special baby: God's son, Jesus. She agrees with little hesitation.

## 12. Walking tall
LUKE 1:39–45

Gabriel tells Mary that her cousin, Elizabeth, is also expecting a miracle baby. Mary travels many miles to visit Elizabeth.

## 13. A song of joy
LUKE 1:46–55

Mary sings out her belief that her child Jesus will be vitally important to God's salvation plan for the whole world.

## 14. Joseph walks out
LUKE 1:56 AND MATTHEW 1:18–19

When Joseph hears about the miraculous baby, he jumps to the obvious, but wrong, conclusion. Mary's obedience to God threatens her relationship with Joseph.

## 15. Walking in the dark
MATTHEW 1:20–23

The first Christmas is tinged with deep pain. Mary has been misunderstood and shunned by Joseph. Her life is in real danger as she stands alone and comfortless.

## 16. Joseph wakes up
MATTHEW 1:24

Where Mary failed, God succeeds: he persuades Joseph in a dream to take on his new role as guardian of the Christ-child.

## 17. Walking up the aisle
MATTHEW 1:25

Mary and Joseph's wedding day must have been a mixture of joyful celebration and quiet secrets that bound the couple closer together in trust.

## 18. Marking time

There is intentionally no Bible reading for this day. The story grows silent. But, as the months passed after Mary and Joseph's marriage, quietly, day by day, a new life was growing in Mary.

## 19. Walking in the starlight
MATTHEW 2:1

Far away in an eastern land, wise men see God's heavenly sign in the night sky and begin their long journey to worship the child born to be king. Their inclusion in the first Christmas is symbolic of God's welcome to all, no matter what race or creed.

## 20. Walking with the shepherds
LUKE 2:8

The shepherds were the social outcasts of their time, yet their inclusion in the Christmas story symbolizes the ministry of Jesus, the good Shepherd, who guides and protects his sheep.

## 21. Walking and talking with God
LUKE 2:36–37

Faithful Anna prayed for many years that God would send a special leader. At last her prayers have been answered.

## 22. No walkover
MATTHEW 2:1

Publicly Herod appears to be a most religious man, yet privately he is an ungodly, murdering tyrant. Herod has religion but no relationship with God.

## 23. Walking to Bethlehem
LUKE 2:1–4

Mary and Joseph have to walk for days to reach Bethlehem when the Roman Emperor Augustus orders everyone to return to their home town to be listed in the record books, but perhaps Luke tells us about the event to show that their journey was part of God's plan.

## 24. Walking the streets
LUKE 2:5–7

If only the villagers had known who Mary and Joseph were, and who the baby was that Mary carried, perhaps they would have made room for them instead of making excuses.

Reproduced with permission from *Walking with Jesus through Advent and Christmas* published by BRF 2005 (1 84101 360 9) www.barnabasinchurches.org.uk

### 25. Resting a while
LUKE 2:6–7
Giving birth to the Son of God in a stable! Was God badly organized? No! With God it was the person, not the place, that made the event special. What symbolism could we attach to the place of Jesus' birth?

### 26. A spring in their step
LUKE 2:8–19
How extraordinary for God to choose outcasts of society—the poor, unpopular shepherds—to be the witnesses and first heralds of Christ's birth.

### 27. Walking into a trap
MATTHEW 2:1–8
On hearing of their mission, Herod plans to use the wise men as bloodhounds to track down the Christ, so that he can send his soldiers to kill him.

### 28. Walking alongside
LUKE 2:22–32 AND 38
The stable in Bethlehem may have filled Mary and Joseph with concern, but the temple in Jerusalem dispels any doubts that their son is, indeed, the longed-for Messiah.

### 29. The hill walkers arrive
MATTHEW 2:9–12
If the wise men are disappointed not to find the Christ-child in Jerusalem, they look with new eyes at the baby lying in his mother's arms, and worship him as God's new king.

### 30. Walking in fear
MATTHEW 2:16–18
It is easy to push this event out of our minds in the midst of the Christmas celebrations, yet it reminds us of the forces of evil that would kill innocent children in the quest to destroy good.

### 31. You'll never walk alone
MATTHEW 2:13–15
Herod's plan to destroy the Christ-child is thwarted when God warns Joseph in a dream to flee to safety in Egypt.

## Mini-map for adults

### 1. Preparation for the journey
LUKE 1:1 AND 3–4
Luke sets out his Gospel by first showing that he has carefully researched the events that surround the truth about Jesus.

### 2. Walking with God
LUKE 3:38
Luke places importance on showing us that Jesus' family tree could be traced back all the way to Adam and then to God.

### 3. A fresh start
LUKE 3:36
Luke includes Noah in the family tree—a farmer who learnt to be a sailor as part of God's first rescue plan.

### 4. Listening to God
LUKE 3:34
In obedience to God, Abraham started a new life and a new family that one day would include people of many faiths—Jewish, Christian and Muslim.

### 5. Ordinary people
LUKE 3:31–32
Abraham's family also included a shepherd boy called David, who became king of God's people Israel.

### 6. A family tree of faith
LUKE 3:23–24
Heli is not famous, but without him the first Christmas would not have taken place.

### 7. God's plan for our lives
LUKE 1:5–7
A year before the first Christmas, God promises Zechariah and Elizabeth that they will have a son, even though they are elderly and childless.

### 8. Walking through God's plan
LUKE 1:8–20
The angel Gabriel is sent by God to announce the news to Zechariah—news so wonderful that the old priest cannot believe it.

Reproduced with permission from *Walking with Jesus through Advent and Christmas* published by BRF 2005
(1 84101 360 9) www.barnabasinchurches.org.uk

# 1 December

## Preparation for the journey

### LUKE 1:1 AND 3–4

 *Many people have tried to tell the story of what God has done among us [in Jesus]... So I made a careful study of everything and then decided to write and tell you exactly what took place... I have done this to let you know the truth about what you have heard [about Jesus].*

### Journey guide

Luke is one of our guides as we explore the events of the first Christmas. He wants to encourage us that faith in Jesus is built on real historical facts. He wants us to know that he has taken great trouble to go back to the places where events took place and find the people who knew Jesus and were eyewitnesses to his amazing life.

Above all, Luke wants us to know that events which seemed to be coincidences—just different things happening in history—were in fact all part of God's great rescue plan for the whole world. The wonderful thing about the Bible is that it's not just a history book about what God has done, but the living word of God, speaking to us and showing us how to prepare for our journey with Jesus.

### Daily travels

Bring to mind a special person or event that helped you think more deeply about God. In what ways might this journey through Advent be another important milestone on your journey of faith?

### The journey in colour

The Bible is the story of the many people who put God at the centre of their lives. Express in colour the lives of so many different people following God.

### Prayer for the journey

 Heavenly Father, thank you for the gift of your word, and for all the people who shared their story so that we too could meet you. Help us to listen and learn so that, through their stories, we may understand more about the real meaning of Christmas. Amen

# 1

# Preparation for the journey

## LUKE 1:3

I made a careful study of everything and then decided to write
and tell you exactly what took place.

# 2 December

## Walking with God

### LUKE 3:38

*The family tree of Jesus went all the way back to Adam and then to God.*

### Journey guide

Luke traces Jesus' *human* family tree back through history to the first 'son of God', whose name was Adam. Jesus' birth was not unplanned; it was the final part of long preparations that took thousands of years in human history to complete.

Jesus is described as the 'second Adam' because he came to put right what went wrong when the first Adam turned his back on God. Jesus shows us what humanity could have been like, if only Adam had remained faithful to God. (You can find out more about the story of Adam in Genesis 1—2.)

### Daily travels

Think about the truth that no birth is unplanned in God's eyes. God created each one of us out of love and for a purpose. We will never know that purpose if we turn our backs on God.

### The journey in colour

Today we see the first of many footprints in our Christmas story-map. Out of the darkness of ancient history we see some of the first human footprints. What colours will you use to celebrate this?

### Prayer for the journey

Creator God, thank you for making us part of your planned creation. Open our hearts to your love and the beauty of your creation. Give us a fresh understanding of what it means to be your child. Amen

# 2

# Walking with God

LUKE 3:38

The family tree of Jesus went all the way back to Adam and then to God.

# 3 December

## A fresh start

LUKE 3:36

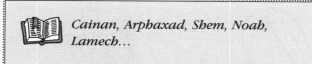

*Cainan, Arphaxad, Shem, Noah, Lamech...*

### Journey guide

After Adam and Eve's disobedience, humanity soon lost its way. People forgot about God and became selfish and greedy, so that those who were powerful became more powerful and those who were powerless became more oppressed. God's beautiful world was in danger of becoming a polluted, exhausted and damaged mess. It was time to start again.

God planned to wash away the mess and start again with just one faithful family. He chose a farmer called Noah. Noah gathered his family and at least one pair of every living creature into the ark, safe from the coming flood. (You can find out more about the story of Noah in Genesis 6—9.)

### Daily travels

Think about your own life. Think about your relationships, your family and your attitude towards God's world. Is there anything that needs to be washed away, or given a fresh start? Don't wait for New Year! Resolve to make a new start today.

### The journey in colour

Add a new picture to your Christmas story-map today. What colour would the damp soil be after a flood? On the water's edge, a rainbow of God's promise is reflected from the sky. Think about the colours red, orange, yellow, green, blue, indigo and violet. What special significance might they have for you?

There are footprints of animals and people on the damp soil as they disembark from the ark. Perhaps the rainbow of God's promise is reflected in their steps?

### Prayer for the journey

Merciful God, forgive us for spoiling the wonderful world you made for us. Forgive us for spoiling our relationships with those around us. Help us to be part of the answer, not the problem, in your world. Help us to make a fresh start with you and with others in your beautiful world. Amen

# 3

# A fresh start

LUKE 3:36

Cainan, Arphaxad, Shem, Noah, Lamech…

# 4 December

## Listening to God

### LUKE 3:34

 *Jacob, Isaac, Abraham, Terah, Nahor...*

### Journey guide

Luke continues his journey through Jesus' family tree. As the centuries pass, we come to a man called Abraham (Abram). Abraham had faith in God, even though he wasn't able to read about him in scripture, meet with him through a local church or learn about him from parents. Abraham was not a religious leader—he was a settled and successful businessman— but he learned to listen to the voice of God's Spirit in his heart. In faith, he made the decision to leave the security of his settled life and go on a long and dangerous journey to the place where he believed God wanted him to be.

Generations later, millions of people look back at Abraham and recognize him as a spiritual leader and the father-figure of faith. (You can find out more about the story of Abraham in Genesis 12—18.)

### Daily travels

We have a great advantage over Abraham in that we have the Bible to teach us about God, telling us the stories of many who have followed God. We also have our local church to support us in our journey of faith. Perhaps we take all this for granted? Abraham spent time with God in prayer. Do we need to invest more time with God, learning the stories of the people of faith and listening to God in prayer?

## The journey in colour

Abraham left his city life to go on an adventure with his whole family, seeking God's will for his life. We see the edge of the city's pavements running out into the desert. What colour do they represent for you?

### Prayer for the journey

 God of new beginnings, help us to spend more time listening to you. Give us wisdom to know when to move on with you, and the courage to keep following you in our adventure of faith.
Amen

# Listening to God

## LUKE 3:34

## Jacob, Isaac, Abraham, Terah, Nahor...

Reproduced with permission from *Walking with Jesus through Advent and Christmas* published by BRF 2005 (1 84101 360 9) **www.barnabasinchurches.org.uk**

# 5 December

## Ordinary people

### LUKE 3:31–32

 *Melea, Menna, Mattatha, Nathan, David, Jesse, Obed, Boaz, Salmon, Nahshon…*

### Journey guide

As Luke continues back along the family tree, we discover a king. Imagine researching your family history and finding that you have royal connections! I wonder how it would feel. King David started life as a humble shepherd-boy, yet he was chosen by God to become Israel's greatest king.

Luke's recording of the family tree reminds us that Jesus, like David, was born into a lowly family. But Jesus and David were very different: David was a warring king with an army of soldiers, whereas Jesus is the 'Prince of Peace' who came to end wars, with his army of followers made up of unarmed men, women and children. (You can find out more about David in 1 and 2 Samuel. His story starts in 1 Samuel 16.)

### Daily travels

Sadly, many people think that they will never do great things for God because they are not 'great' people—famous, rich or powerful. But the Bible shows us time and again that God works with ordinary people, helping them to do great things. Perhaps 'great' people rely on their own strength, whereas 'ordinary' people rely on God?

### The journey in colour

Today we see the footsteps of David the shepherd boy, as he leaves his sheep to take up his crown and become king of Israel. How might you express in colour David's experience of leading his flock and his subsequent role as the leader of God's people?

---

### Prayer for the journey

 Loving God, help us to see how much you care for ordinary people. Ever-living God, we invite you to work through us, in the ordinariness of our daily lives, to do extraordinary things. Amen

---

# Ordinary people

## LUKE 3:31–32

Melea, Menna, Mattatha, Nathan, David, Jesse,
Obed, Boaz, Salmon, Nahshon…

# 6 December

---○─( 6 )─○---

## A family tree of faith

### LUKE 3:23–24

 *When Jesus began to preach, he was about thirty years old. Everyone thought he was the son of Joseph. But his family went back through Heli, Matthat, Levi, Melchi, Jannai, Joseph…*

### Journey guide

Who was Heli? Why, out of all the people in the family tree, have we stopped here? First of all because, without Heli, Jesus' family tree would not have been complete: he is as important in Jesus' family tree as King David. Secondly because Heli would have prepared the way for Jesus simply by the fact that he passed down the story of faith to the next generation. And thirdly because he was the father of Joseph. For all three reasons, he is a very important person in the story of Christmas, even though his name is little-known.

### Daily travels

In many ways it is more important simply to pass on what we know about God than it is to do something impressive. If Heli had not passed on his faith to his son, Joseph would not have had the faith to trust that God was doing something new and wonderful. If we do not pass on our faith, our Christian family tree will die with us. What a gift we have to pass on: the gift of friendship with our God.

### The journey in colour

In the ancient world, the scriptures would have been written on long rolls of parchment, which enabled one generation to pass on their faith accurately to the next. Heli and his son Joseph would have read scrolls containing the scriptures in the synagogue. What colour would best express the scriptures for you against the background of the barren desert sands?

### Prayer for the journey

 Loving God, forgive us when we forget how important each and every one of us is to you. Help us to see that our lives are important to your great plan. Help us to recognize that other people are important to you, however ordinary they may seem. Amen

# A family tree of faith

LUKE 3:23–24

When Jesus began to preach, he was about thirty years old... his family
went back through Heli, Matthat, Levi, Melchi, Jannai, Joseph...

# 7 December

─────── ○ ⑦ ○ ───────

## God's plan for our lives

### LUKE 1:5–7

 *When Herod was king of Judea, there was a priest called Zechariah from the priestly group of Abijah. His wife Elizabeth was from the family of Aaron. Both of them were good people and pleased the Lord God by obeying all that he had commanded. But they did not have children. Elizabeth could not have any, and both Zechariah and Elizabeth were already old.*

### Journey guide

Luke begins his account of Jesus' life by introducing us to two elderly people who are seemingly at the end of their lives. These two had prayed for a child for years without success. After all that time, they had probably given up hope. In those days, not only was it very sad for a couple to be childless, but it also laid them open to blame, as children were seen to be a sign of God's blessing. In this way, the first Christmas story begins not with hope but with hopelessness, not with joy but with sadness. But, at what seems to be the end of life for these two, God is poised to bring about a new beginning.

### Daily travels

Think about those things in your life that seem to represent 'failed prayer'. Is it possible to believe that God's plans might be beyond your wildest dreams? Prayerfully, invite God to work out his plans for your life.

### The journey in colour

What colours are emptiness and sadness? You will need these colours today. The two sets of footprints belong to Elizabeth and Zechariah. Inside each life is an empty space of childlessness as they walk with God.

---

### Prayer for the journey

 Lord of all our prayers, thank you for listening. Help us to trust you with our lives and our plans. Keep hope alive in our hearts and in our prayers. Amen

---

# God's plan for our lives

LUKE 1:7

Elizabeth could not have [children], and both Zechariah
and Elizabeth were already old.

Reproduced with permission from *Walking with Jesus through Advent and Christmas* published by BRF 2005 (1 84101 360 9) www.barnabasinchurches.org.uk

# 8 December

○ **8** ○

## Walking through God's plan

### LUKE 1:8–20

> *One day Zechariah's group of priests were on duty [inside the temple]... while the people stood outside praying. All at once an angel from the Lord appeared to Zechariah... (He) was confused and afraid when he saw the angel. But the angel told him, 'Don't be afraid, Zechariah! God has heard your prayers. Your wife Elizabeth will have a son, and you must name him John... Your son will be a great servant of the Lord... John will lead many people in Israel to turn back to the Lord their God... John will get people ready for the Lord.' Zechariah said to the angel, 'How will I know this is going to happen? My wife and I are both very old.' The angel answered, 'I am Gabriel, God's servant, and I was sent to tell you this good news. You have not believed what I have said. So you will not be able to say a thing until all this happens. But everything will take place when it is supposed to.'*

### Journey guide

Have you ever complained to God about his timing? Things happen too soon or too slowly, or prayers never seem to be answered. Childlessness had left an emptiness in Zechariah's and Elizabeth's lives—an emptiness of unanswered prayers, which perhaps felt like a silent 'no' from God. Many of us can relate to the emptiness of long-unanswered prayers—about sickness, money or direction for the future.

Suddenly God steps into Zechariah's life, but Zechariah feels it is too late. God has waited too long.

He has made a difficult request impossible. However, the angel Gabriel is not apologetic. Rather, he is annoyed with Zechariah: God is never late; he is the Lord of all time. God is always on time.

Praying for immediate action is like demanding that the baker should open the oven and give you your Christmas cake when it's only half-baked. Gabriel knew that Zechariah's prayers were being answered just at the right time for God's bigger plans.

### Daily travels

Carefully consider the way you approach God in prayer. Do you treat God as if he were a pizza delivery boy? Or are you offering your life to God for him to use in his own time and planning?

### The journey in colour

On the story-map today, Zechariah's footsteps stop because he cannot see the way ahead. But the angel Gabriel shows him God's way—beyond his hopes, but not beyond God's power. Angels in the Bible are bright messengers of God who often amazed and terrified people with their size and brightness. How will you colour the picture today?

### Prayer for the journey

 Lord of all time, help us to find peace in the busyness when time seems to be racing by. Help us to find hope in the emptiness when time seems to drag. Lord of all time, help us to spend our time wisely with you. Amen

# 8

# Walking through God's plan

LUKE 1:11

All at once an angel from the Lord appeared to Zechariah.

# 9 December

**9**

## Reading between the lines

### JOHN 21:25

 *Jesus did many other things. If they were all written in books I don't suppose there would be room enough in the whole world for all the books.*

### Journey guide

God is preparing so many things all at once, in different places, with different people, that Matthew and Luke have to leave some things out. To see the whole story of Jesus we need to read between the lines of all four Gospels. Like a dot-to-dot puzzle, we need to join up the four accounts in order to make the puzzle clear. For example, Matthew and Luke never mention the fact that Joseph was a carpenter, but by reading the whole of the life of Jesus in all four Gospels we can piece the story together and find out more than we are told in the Christmas narratives alone.

### Journey guide

While the angel Gabriel was visiting the old priest Zechariah, in a small village far away an ordinary man called Joseph was working in a dusty carpentry shed. However, his mind was not on his work. He was planning his forthcoming marriage to his fiancée, Mary. Joseph was not a priest or religious leader, yet God chose him to be the earthly guardian of Jesus, the Son of God.

### Daily travels

Pause to think about the way you read the Bible. Perhaps sometimes you get a little lost. It's not always easy to join the pieces together. This Advent, set yourself the challenge of reading all four Gospels—Matthew, Mark, Luke and John—and put together the 'big picture' of Jesus' story of salvation.

### The journey in colour

Today we add Joseph to the Christmas story-map, working at his carpentry bench among the wood shavings and tools. Joseph was dreaming of his wedding as he worked, with no notion of the adventure ahead. How might this be expressed in colour?

### Prayer for the journey

 Heavenly Father, when things seem confusing in life, give us hope not to lose heart. Help us to see the signs of your great plan. Join our lives to yours through the unity of your Holy Spirit. Amen

★ ★ ★ ★ ★ ★ ★ ★ ★ ★ ★ ★ ★ ★ ★ ★ ★ ★ ★ ★ ★ ★ ★ ★ ★ ★ ★ ★ ★ ★ ★ ★ ★ ★ ★ ★ ★ ★ ★ ★ ★ ★ ★ ★ ★ ★ ★ ★ ★

# Reading between the lines

### JOHN 21:25

Jesus did many other things. If they were all written in books I don't suppose there would be room enough in the whole world for all the books.

# 10 December

## Promises, promises

### LUKE 2:5

 *Mary was engaged to Joseph...*

### Journey guide

Long before Mary and Joseph entered the story in Luke's account, they had made a promise to each other that bound them together for life. Their relationship would be tested to breaking point in the following months with the shocking news of Mary's pregnancy. There would be questions about broken promises and meetings with angels—even perhaps doubts about their grip on reality.

There were so many things that could have torn their relationship apart, so it is important for us to remember that Mary and Joseph were ordinary people of their time, making plans to build a life together, with all the worries that this brings for any engaged couple. Soon Joseph and Mary would be drawn into the events of that first Christmas. Caught up in the story, it is easy to miss the deep, forgiving spiritual nature of their love for each other. Their story is one of the most romantic love stories of all time and an inspiration to all those who are planning marriage, or who are already married.

### Daily travels

Think about promises you have made. Are those promises too fragile to stand the test of time, or are they strong enough and forgiving enough to survive the storms and shocks of life?

### The journey in colour

Today we celebrate Mary and Joseph's engagement and forthcoming marriage. It is a day of happiness, songs and promises, surrounded by family and friends. No one has any idea of the events that will change the carefully laid plans. Colour the picture to express the celebration, but what colours will you use to hint at the hard times ahead?

### Prayer for the journey

 Lord of all promises, we thank you for all who are bound to us in love. Melt our brittle love that breaks so easily. Grow in us a deeper, more forgiving love for others. Amen

# 10

# Promises, promises

LUKE 2:5

Mary was engaged to Joseph...

# 11 December

 **11**

## God-bearer

LUKE 1:26–38

 *God sent the angel Gabriel to the town of Nazareth in Galilee with a message for a virgin named Mary... The angel greeted Mary and said, 'You are truly blessed! The Lord is with you.' Mary was confused by the angel's words and wondered what they meant. Then the angel told Mary, 'Don't be afraid! God is pleased with you, and you will have a son. His name will be Jesus. He will be great and will be called the Son of God Most High... He will rule the people of Israel for ever, and his kingdom will never end.' Mary asked the angel, 'How can this happen? I am not married!' The angel answered, 'The Holy Spirit will come down to you, and God's power will come over you. So your child will be called the holy Son of God. Your relative Elizabeth is also going to have a son, even though she is old. No one thought she could ever have a baby, but in three months she will have a son. Nothing is impossible for God!' Mary said, 'I am the Lord's servant! Let it happen as you have said.'*

### Journey guide

If Zechariah had been shocked, Mary was overwhelmed to hear that God wanted to involve an ordinary person such as herself in his world-changing plans. The angel Gabriel's news was so unexpected and so amazing that it was hard fully to understand God's plans. God wanted Mary to be the mother of the most special child of all time. This child was not conceived from a human father, but born of God. No one could have prepared

Mary for the news the angel brought, because God was doing something new—something that had never before been accomplished. The Old Testament scriptures speak of God's power and glory; now, in Jesus, he would show himself as a gentle God. Mary is to hold the vulnerable smallness of God in her arms. He is just as holy, but less remote.

### Daily travels

In the Orthodox Church, Mary is known as the 'God-bearer'—the person who carried God. Carrying a baby changes the way people respond to you. God invites us to be 'God-bearers', to carry the divine new life of God around with us everywhere we go. Imagine how that could change the way people react to us.

### The journey in colour

Mary's life is lit up by the angel Gabriel, who explains how God the Holy Spirit will overshadow her as she receives Jesus into her life. While Mary is carrying Jesus in her womb, the tiny growing imprints of Jesus can be seen in Mary's life. Colour these and the outline of Mary in bright yellow to mark out the light of Christ, and think about the life of Christ entering into our story-map.

---

### Prayer for the journey

Almighty God who created all that is in the universe, help us to welcome you in a new way; help us to receive Jesus into our lives, and help us to bring your new life to others. Amen

---

# God-bearer

LUKE 1:26

God sent the angel Gabriel to the town of Nazareth
in Galilee with a message for a virgin named Mary...

# 12 December

**○ (12) ○**

## Walking tall

### LUKE 1:39–45

 *Mary hurried to a town in the hill country of Judea. She went into Zechariah's home, where she greeted Elizabeth. When Elizabeth heard Mary's greeting, her baby moved within her. The Holy Spirit came upon Elizabeth. Then in a loud voice she said to Mary: 'God has blessed you more than any other woman! … As soon as I heard your greeting, my baby became happy and moved within me. The Lord has blessed you because you believed that he will keep his promise.'*

## Journey guide

Perhaps Mary must have felt very much alone as she adjusted to the reality of her pregnancy. We too can often feel alone when faced with personal dilemmas. Often, God gives us others to help and support us, but sometimes it's up to us to make the effort to meet them.

Mary had to make a journey of at least 50 miles across dangerous hill country in order to meet Elizabeth. It must have taken great courage and determination for a young woman to make such a journey, and then to share her excitement over what God was doing in her life. Did Mary worry about what kind of reaction she would get? Would Elizabeth turn her away in shame or fear? No! Mary received a warm welcome from this older woman. At a time when other people would perhaps have criticized or not understood, Mary found support and understanding from someone very different in age, but who was experiencing similarly wonderful things from God.

## Daily travels

God doesn't want us to feel alone or try to find our way through life without support from others. Sadly, fears and worries can stop us from reaching out to find the support we need. Let Mary be an inspiration to encourage us to make a journey through our worries, to find fellowship with someone who will understand what God is doing in our life.

## The journey in colour

Mary and Elizabeth walk closely together, closing the gap between all the things that divided them in life as they encouraged each other in their adventure with God. The light of the Christ-child glows gently in Mary.

### Prayer for the journey

 Heavenly Father, you know all the fears that make us feel alone. Show us how to find the support we need. Give us courage to reach out and support someone else. Lord, overcome our worries with your loving hope. Amen

# Walking tall

LUKE 1:41

**When Elizabeth heard Mary's greeting, her baby moved within her.**

Reproduced with permission from *Walking with Jesus through Advent and Christmas* published by BRF 2005 (1 84101 360 9) www.barnabasinchurches.org.uk

# 13 December

### ─● (13) ●─

## A song of joy

### LUKE 1:46–55

>  *[After Elizabeth had greeted her] Mary said, 'With all my heart I praise the Lord, and I am glad because of God my Saviour. He cares for me, his humble servant. From now on, all people will say God has blessed me. God All-Powerful has done great things for me, and his name is holy. He always shows mercy to everyone who worships him. The Lord has used his powerful arm to scatter those who are proud. He drags strong rulers from their thrones and puts humble people in places of power. God gives the hungry good things to eat, and sends the rich away with nothing. He helps his servant Israel and is always merciful to his people. The Lord made this promise to our ancestors, to Abraham and his family for ever!'*

### Journey guide

Mary's heart has been like a river that has been stopped up with fear, but now it is released. Mary bursts out with praise to her God. On her long journey, maybe Mary remembered Hannah, the mother of the great prophet Samuel (1 Samuel 1:1—2:10). Mary sings out with excitement that God will right the many wrongs that poor people suffer at the hands of oppressive rich rulers.

Listen again to Mary's song. Can you hear the same passion in the songs of young people today who sing out the feelings of their hearts? It's a song of joy from the heart of an ordinary young person who is so excited to be caught up in God's plans.

### Daily travels

The Bible has much to say about God's heart for those who are poor in body, mind and spirit. As our love for God grows, so does our desire to do the things that are on God's heart. In the busyness of Christmas preparations, God lays on our hearts the desire to be part of his plan to help those who are poor in body, mind and spirit.

### The journey in colour

On our story-map today, the big footprint reflects the rainbow in the sky above. This is a sign from God that he will come among his people in a new way. What colours express this thought?

### Prayer for the journey

Living Lord, thank you that you fill our hearts with love and hope. Help us to express the joy of knowing you. Show us how to share that joy in practical ways with those who are poor in body, mind or spirit. May our lives be like Mary's song—full of love and joy. Amen

# 13

# A song of joy

## LUKE 1:46

Mary said: 'With all my heart I praise the Lord,
and I am glad because of God my Saviour.'

Reproduced with permission from *Walking with Jesus through Advent and Christmas* published by BRF 2005 (1 84101 360 9) www.barnabasinchurches.org.uk

# 14 December

## Joseph walks out

### LUKE 1:56 AND MATTHEW 1:18–19

 *Mary stayed with Elizabeth about three months. Then she went back home.*

*Mary was engaged to Joseph from King David's family. But before they were married, she learnt that she was going to have a baby by God's Holy Spirit. Joseph was a good man and did not want to embarrass Mary in front of everyone. So he decided to call off the wedding quietly.*

### Journey guide

It would be easy to see Joseph as the heartless boyfriend, but that would not be fair. In ordinary circumstances, Joseph would have been absolutely right to believe that this baby was the result of a secret affair with another man. But there was no other man, only God. Broken-hearted Joseph jumped to the wrong conclusion.

In this situation, the Jewish law expected the man to leave the woman who had broken her promise. Joseph went off to struggle in an agony of indecision between his deep love for Mary and his duty to his faith. Everyone would congratulate him on the birth of his son, but Joseph would always wonder who the secret father was: was he a neighbour, a friend? Joseph felt hurt, betrayed and even angry. How could Mary think that he would believe such an incredible story? Did she think he was that stupid?

### Daily travels

It's too easy to jump to conclusions and point the finger of blame. Try to see things from another person's point of view today. Try to stand in their shoes and see the world from their viewpoint. Perhaps this will change your feelings about a situation that you are finding difficult or painful.

### The journey in colour

Today our story-map shows Mary walking on in God's plan. The light of Christ glows gently in her, while Joseph walks in the opposite direction. Think about times when you have felt hurt or betrayed. How might you express this in colour? How might you express flashes of anger or the darkness of betrayal?

### Prayer for the journey

 Heavenly Father, help us to see the world through other people's eyes and walk through the world in their shoes. Give us the gift of understanding. Amen

# 14

# Joseph walks out

## MATTHEW 1:19

Joseph… decided to call off the wedding quietly.

# 15 December

## Walking in the dark

### MATTHEW 1:20–23

 *While Joseph was thinking about this, an angel of the Lord came to him in a dream. The angel said, 'Joseph, the baby that Mary will have is from the Holy Spirit. Go ahead and marry her. Then after her baby is born, name him Jesus, because he will save his people from their sins.' So the Lord's promise came true, just as the prophet had said, 'A virgin will have a baby boy, and he will be called Immanuel,' which means 'God is with us.'*

### Journey guide

This is a dark moment in the Christmas story. Joseph went away to think by himself, leaving Mary all alone. This must have been a terrifying time for her. No doubt she thought about how people would misunderstand the situation and how she would be blamed and punished. Did Mary wonder if it was all going wrong? Where was God when she needed him most?

Although Mary felt alone, God had not left her. He was hard at work, finding a way to get through to Joseph. People listen to God in different ways—some in pictures, others in stories. Perhaps Joseph couldn't hear God in the same way as Mary did, so God spoke to him in a dream, quietly but powerfully—the kind of dream that is just as real on waking. While God was talking to Joseph in his dreams, Mary must have felt as if her dreams had turned to nightmares. Being part of God's plan can be exciting, but it can also be scary.

### Daily travels

Following Jesus is not always easy. Sometimes our obedience to God can be misunderstood by others and we can feel very much alone. No one seems to understand or believe us. However, we can be assured that God will never abandon us when we are obedient to his will. Unseen, but ever present, he is working for good.

### The journey in colour

The story-map has reached a dark day. In the picture, Mary's footsteps still follow God's plans, perhaps timidly now as she is surrounded by the darkness of worries. The light of Jesus glows faintly in her life.

---

### Prayer for the journey

 Heavenly Father, help us to talk to you about the things that worry us. Help us to know that you are with us in the darkness. When we cannot see a way ahead, call us by name into the safety of your love. Amen

---

# 15

# Walking in the dark

MATTHEW 1:20

While Joseph was thinking about this, an angel of the
Lord came to him in a dream.

# 16 December

## Joseph wakes up

MATTHEW 1:24

 *After Joseph woke up, he and Mary were soon married, just as the Lord's angel had told him to do.*

### Journey guide

The Christmas story is so well known that it is easy to forget that things might have been very different if Joseph had left Mary and married someone else. Joseph woke up, not only to a new day but also to a new understanding. The angel of God had woken Joseph up to God's great plan. However, all God's efforts could have been wasted if Joseph had been too proud to acknowledge that he had made an error of judgment. It is because Joseph realized that he had an important part to play in supporting Mary in God's big rescue plan that the Christmas story is the one we know so well.

Joseph reminds us of another Joseph—Jacob's favourite son (Genesis 37). God also spoke to this Joseph in a dream. Both Josephs remind us that our dreams can be a place for us to meet with God. (If we have bad dreams, we can invite God to give us his peace.)

### Daily travels

We may feel that we have known quite a lot about God for years, but have never fitted everything together. One day we may wake up to know God in a special friendship of faith and listen to him with a new understanding. Like Joseph, every one of us has a special part to play in God's great plan, which we will find out only by following Jesus. Now that's an adventure!

### The journey in colour

We are about halfway through our Advent story-map. The angel leads Joseph back to Mary. What colours show this happy point in their lives as, once again, with new understanding, they plan their future life together?

### Prayer for the journey

 Creator God, help us to know that you are with us whether we are awake or asleep. We welcome you into our dreams and ask you to drive away our nightmares. Protect us with your angel bodyguards as we sleep, so that on waking we might follow Jesus in all we do. Amen

# 16

# Joseph wakes up

MATTHEW 1:24

After Joseph woke up, he and Mary were soon married…

Reproduced with permission from *Walking with Jesus through Advent and Christmas* published by BRF 2005 (1 84101 360 9) www.barnabasinchurches.org.uk

# 17 December

## Walking up the aisle

### MATTHEW 1:25

 *[Mary and Joseph] did not sleep together before her baby was born.*

### Journey guide

Most weddings are times of celebration—a new beginning for the happy couple. A wedding is a very public party with everyone sharing the happy day. In obedience to God, Joseph went ahead with the wedding that he and Mary had planned before God had intervened with the strange news of a special baby. But it must have been a difficult situation for the couple. Outwardly they must have seemed like any normal, nervous wedding couple, but inwardly only they and God knew the secret they kept as they prepared themselves for the arrival of God's special and mysterious baby. This secret bound them tightly together in faithfulness and trust.

### Daily travels

Advent reminds us that what was once the greatest secret in the world is now the greatest public party and celebration in the world. Think about how we can share the secret of Jesus among our friends and neighbours this Christmas.

### The journey in colour

Jewish wedding ceremonies took place at night, so Mary and Joseph's footsteps would have been lit by candles and oil lamps as they were surrounded by family, friends and neighbours. What colours show the public wedding and the wonderful secret they kept?

### Prayer for the journey

Heavenly Father, help us not to keep Jesus a secret that we are afraid to share with anyone. Give us the courage to let Jesus show in our lives, in our friendships and our forgiveness of others. Amen

# 17

# Walking up the aisle

## MATTHEW 1:25

[Mary and Joseph] did not sleep together before her baby was born.

# 18 December

 **18**

## Marking time

There is intentionally no Bible reading for this day.

### Journey guide

Luke wrote his Gospel from the accounts of people who knew Jesus, perhaps even Mary herself. There were, no doubt, so many stories that Luke could not include everything. There is no reading today because there is a gap in the Christmas story. From the time when Joseph agreed to go ahead with the wedding until their journey to Bethlehem, Luke gives us no further information, for the simple reason that nothing dramatic happened. As we too pause in the story today, it is important to remember that when Mary allowed God into her life, even though at first nothing outwardly seemed to be happening, inwardly the new life was growing daily stronger within her.

### Daily travels

Obedience to God is simply saying 'yes' to God. Things can often seem very quiet, when nothing seems to be happening outwardly for months and months. Yet, if we allow it, God's new life will develop within us and our faith will grow. Meeting with other Christians is a natural and important way to share our experience of God and help our faith to grow.

### The journey in colour

Today we add a difficult time to our story-map. As Mary patiently awaits the birth of her special baby, what colours express the months of waiting while the life of God grows in her?

---

**Prayer for the journey**

 Lord of all time, be with us when time drags like a heavy weight. Be with us when time slips through our fingers like sand. Sometimes we are so impatient, sometimes so fearful. Lord of all time, teach us to live every moment, not looking backwards or forwards but living in your presence now. Amen

---

# Marking time

*There is intentionally no Bible reading for this day.*

Reproduced with permission from *Walking with Jesus through Advent and Christmas* published by BRF 2005 (1 84101 360 9) www.barnabasinchurches.org.uk

# 19 December

## Walking in the starlight

### MATTHEW 2:1

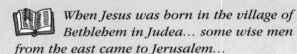

*When Jesus was born in the village of Bethlehem in Judea... some wise men from the east came to Jerusalem...*

### Journey guide

Long before Mary and Joseph began their journey to Bethlehem, other travellers had set out on an adventure, weeks, maybe months before. The most mysterious characters in the Christmas story are the wise men, or Magi, who came from a country far in the east, perhaps Babylon. They were foreigners with a different language and different traditions. They set out on a dangerous adventure in search of a baby born to be king. If we didn't know the end of the story, we might wonder about their chances of succeeding in their mission. They had no name or address to guide them. To make it more difficult, Mary and Joseph were an ordinary, unknown couple and—to make it really impossible—Mary and Joseph were not known in Bethlehem. The chances of success were very, very small. The story of the wise men reminds Christians that many people are on the Christmas journey. This is a time to welcome people who are different from us on their journey to meet Jesus.

### Daily travels

In your community, who do you think God is calling and welcoming this Christmas? Perhaps they live a different kind of life or speak another language, yet God is their Father and he is guiding them to meet Jesus amid the Christmas celebrations. Think about how we too can welcome others this Christmas.

### The journey in colour

The wise men's camels leave sets of hoof prints as they climb mountains and cross dry plains on the long journey. The star is reflected in the stream as it guides them in the right direction. What colours reflect their feelings as they travel, and what colour is the reflected star?

### Prayer for the journey

Heavenly Father, thank you that we are all your children. This Christmas, help us to welcome those who are different from us. Knit us together as a community and show us how to help others to meet Jesus. Amen

# 19

# Walking in the starlight

MATTHEW 2:1

Some wise men from the east came to Jerusalem...

# 20 December

## Walking with the shepherds

### LUKE 2:8

 *That night in the fields near Bethlehem some shepherds were guarding their sheep.*

### Journey guide

It's important to remember that the shepherds, like others who were part of the Christmas story, were just getting on with their ordinary lives: they were not rehearsing their parts as if in a nativity play. But God chose to bring these ordinary people into his amazing rescue plan. Shepherds in Israel had a bad reputation. People shunned them. They were considered to be unclean (and probably stank of sheep), so they would be the very last people to be invited into your home. They lived in the open and slept rough in order to guard their flocks against attacking animals or thieves. Because their lives were so different from those of ordinary men and women (and perhaps because they were awake while others slept), they were regarded with distrust and suspected of being thieves and robbers. Treated like outcasts, their lives were sad and lonely.

### Daily travels

Christmas celebrates the birth of the Son of God, who reaches out to those who are treated like outcasts and reminds them that they are precious to God. Who in your community is treated like an outcast? What will you do about it?

### The journey in colour

Today's picture is covered with the hoof prints of a large flock of sheep. Among them are the footprints of the shepherds. The shepherds were so poor that they had holes in their shoes, or no shoes at all. What colour expresses the feelings of the shepherds?

### Prayer for the journey

Heavenly Father, thank you for sending Jesus to everyone who feels like an outcast. Help us to know that we are accepted as much as anyone else. Help us to pass on the good news of Jesus by accepting others just as you do. Amen

# 20

# Walking with the shepherds

LUKE 2:8

That night in the fields near Bethlehem some shepherds
were guarding their sheep.

Reproduced with permission from *Walking with Jesus through Advent and Christmas* published by BRF 2005 (1 84101 360 9) www.barnabasinchurches.org.uk

# 21 December

**– ◦⟨21⟩◦ –**

## Walking and talking with God

### LUKE 2:36–37

 *The prophet Anna was also there in the temple. She was the daughter of Phanuel from the tribe of Asher, and she was very old. In her youth she had been married for seven years, but her husband had died. And now she was eighty-four years old. Night and day she served God in the temple by praying and often going without eating.*

### Journey guide

Years before Joseph and Mary were married, there were faithful people praying that God would send someone special to release his people from the bullying of other countries. It's easy for us to read the Christmas story and think that God answered these prayers three verses later! However, the truth was that godly people like Anna had prayed faithfully day and night at the temple, without any light of hope in their darkness, for years and years. While Anna was praying, little could she know that all the pieces of God's great jigsaw were falling into place. The angels had delivered their secret messages, the wise men were on their way, and Mary and Joseph were about to leave Nazareth and journey to Bethlehem. Not knowing this, Anna kept praying faithfully for God to come and rescue her people and, although she did not know it at the time, God was about to reward her.

### Daily travels

It's easy to give up praying if we do not see something happening. Anna is a great example for us to pray persistently, even when there are no positive signs.

### The journey in colour

Our story-map takes us inside the temple, where we see the special seven-branched candlestick or *menorah*. The night is closing in and Anna's footprints are wearing out the floor as she continues to pray for her people day and night.

### Prayer for the journey

Listening God, thank you for the example of Anna. Grow in us the strength to keep praying, even when we see no change for good. Keep us from giving up and giving in to despair. Listening God, thank you for listening quietly to our prayers. Amen

# 21

# Walking and talking with God

LUKE 2:36

The prophet Anna was also there in the temple.

# 22 December

## No walkover

### MATTHEW 2:1

 *When Jesus was born in the village of Bethlehem in Judea, Herod was king.*

### Journey guide

It's easy to think of King Herod as the Bible's version of Captain Hook, the larger-than-life bully of little children. However, King Herod really was a nasty piece of work. He murdered anyone who got in his way, including members of his own family. As the Christmas story gets closer to the birth of Jesus, it also draws closer to the most dangerous, cunning and powerful person in Israel. Yet publicly King Herod was a very religious man. He was building the largest temple the capital had ever seen. Herod might build a great temple for God, but he refused to invite God into his own heart. His religion was just for show.

Herod reminds us of the very real threat to the people of God in our world. Even people who outwardly appear very religious can, in their hearts, be enemies of God and his people.

### Daily travels

Herod reminds us to pray for our leaders, since even the most religious of our leaders can privately shut God out of their hearts. As followers of Jesus, we need to be wise about whom we trust, and should look for godliness in the daily lives of our leaders.

### The journey in colour

Look closely at the direction of Herod's feet and those of his soldiers and then look back at the whole of God's great story-map. Herod was opposed to God's plan and would try to block the way. However, God's angels are more powerful; nothing can get in their way. What colours might you use to express the goodness of God and the opposition of King Herod?

### Prayer for the journey

King of kings, we pray for our leaders and for all who have power over our lives for good or evil. We pray that they would put their trust in you and walk in the footsteps of Jesus. Protect our leaders and help them not to forget their duty to serve others. Give them loving and forgiving hearts. Amen

# 22

# No walkover

MATTHEW 2:1

When Jesus was born in the village of Bethlehem in Judea, Herod was king.

Reproduced with permission from *Walking with Jesus through Advent and Christmas* published by BRF 2005 (1 84101 360 9) www.barnabasinchurches.org.uk

# 23 December

○─ **23** ─○

## Walking to Bethlehem

### LUKE 2:1–4

>  *About that time Emperor Augustus gave orders for the names of all the people to be listed in record books. These first records were made when Quirinius was governor of Syria. Everyone had to go to their own home town to be listed. So Joseph had to leave Nazareth in Galilee and go to Bethlehem in Judea. Long ago Bethlehem had been King David's home town, and Joseph went there because he was from David's family.*

### Journey guide

Luke reminds us that even the most powerful person in the world is not more powerful than God. The Roman Emperor Augustus was the most powerful person in Mary and Joseph's world. When he gave an order, the whole empire had to obey. However, Augustus was unknowingly doing exactly what God had planned.

Just at the time when she wanted to rest, Mary had to set out on an exhausting journey of some 70 miles. If we are tired out by the crowds in the busy run-up to Christmas, let's spare a thought for Mary and Joseph, who had to travel by foot on that long, long journey, only to find themselves caught up in the crowds when they arrived in Bethlehem. Augustus thought himself so great that he named the month of August after himself. However, the child that Mary carried was even greater. He would make such an impact on the world that we would count our whole calendar by his birth, with the letters AD, or *Anno Domini*, meaning 'in the year of our Lord'.

### Daily travels

It's worth remembering that whoever we have to respect as our leader, teacher, boss or superior, God is in ultimate control.

### The journey in colour

Look carefully at the confusion of footprints in the sand and dirt of the dusty roads, as crowds of people walk in different directions to reach their home towns. What colours will you use to show the busyness of the road? Don't forget to colour Mary's footsteps yellow to show that she is carrying Jesus.

> ### Prayer for the journey
>
>  Lord of all, help us to remember that you are in control of everything. When we feel that we have no freedom and others are in ultimate control of our lives, help us to remember that you are Lord of all, great and small. Thank you, God, that you haven't forgotten us in your plans. Amen

★ ★ ★ ★ ★ ★ ★ ★ ★ ★ ★ ★ ★ ★ ★ ★ ★ ★ ★ ★ ★ ★ ★ ★ ★ ★ ★ ★ ★ ★ ★ ★ ★ ★ ★ ★ ★ ★ ★ ★ ★ ★ ★ ★ ★

# 23

# Walking to Bethlehem

LUKE 2:4

Joseph had to leave Nazareth in Galilee and go to Bethlehem in Judea.

Reproduced with permission from *Walking with Jesus through Advent and Christmas* published by BRF 2005 (1 84101 360 9) www.barnabasinchurches.org.uk

# 24 December

## Walking the streets

### LUKE 2:5–7

 *Mary was engaged to Joseph and travelled with him to Bethlehem. She was soon going to have a baby... [but] there was no room for them in the inn.*

### Journey guide

Normally, babies, rather than parents, choose the exact moment of their arrival, and Mary and Joseph would probably have been very worried that they would not get to Bethlehem in time. No doubt they were relieved to have reached their destination, but then imagine their frustration in not finding anywhere to stay. Joseph, unable to help Mary, must have run from house to house, asking, begging and pleading for some sympathy for his exhausted, frightened and helpless wife. If only the people of Bethlehem had known who this child was, surely they would have given Mary and Joseph the best room in the village and put a memorial plate on the door to remember the occasion. Sadly, no one knew that the baby was the most important person who would ever stay in their village, so no one helped.

### Daily travels

How many people will not find room for the holy family this Christmas? In all the busyness of the run-up to Christmas, let us leave some room for Jesus. How sad to be so busy that we turn God away!

### The journey in colour

Mary's footsteps are smaller as she finds it more difficult to walk. In the doorways, people turn the couple away. What colours would you use to show Joseph's frustration? Remember to colour Mary's footsteps in yellow to show the path God takes in the story-map.

---

### Prayer for the journey

Father of all kindness, you always have time to listen; you always have space in your heart. Make space in our lives for others. Expand our small hearts so that no one is left out. Loving Lord, never let us turn you away. Amen

# 24

# Walking the streets

LUKE 2:5

Mary was engaged to Joseph and travelled with him to Bethlehem.

# 25 December

## Resting a while

### LUKE 2:6–7

*While they were [in Bethlehem], she gave birth to her firstborn son. She dressed him in baby clothes and laid him on a bed of hay...*

### Journey guide

Who could have blamed Joseph and Mary if they had questioned God's plans for them? Far from home, cold and uncomfortable, it would have been quite natural to complain under such circumstances. But Mary doesn't complain. She lays her baby in a borrowed manger and improvises with a bed of hay.

The borrowed manger is a good illustration of Jesus' whole life. As a grown man, he made the comment that 'the Son of Man doesn't have a place to call his own' (Luke 9:58). Laid to sleep in a borrowed manger at his birth, he was laid to rest in a borrowed tomb at his death. He was born, he lived and he died without a place to call home. Only after the miracle of Easter did he finally return to the place where he belonged—the heavenly home from where he had come.

### Daily travels

Christmas is a good time to remember those who are homeless in our towns and cities. Perhaps we can support the people and charities that care for those who have serious problems and no place to call their own.

### The journey in colour

Our story-map has reached the heart of Christmas. Mary, Joseph, animals and angels are gathered around the manger in adoration of this holy birth. Colour the picture and add your own footprints to the scene. Where do you put yourself in the picture?

### Prayer for the journey

All-seeing God, forgive us when we complain and lose sight of your great plan for our lives. Help us, like Mary, to get on humbly with the task in hand. Give us welcoming hearts for those who have nowhere to call home, and grateful hearts for the promise of a place in your heavenly home. Amen

# 25

# Resting a while

LUKE 2:7

[Mary] gave birth to her firstborn son. She dressed him in baby clothes
and laid him on a bed of hay...

# 26 December

───● **26** ●───

## A spring in their step

### LUKE 2:8–19

 *That night in the fields near Bethlehem some shepherds were guarding their sheep. All at once an angel came down to them from the Lord, and the brightness of the Lord's glory flashed around them. The shepherds were frightened. But the angel said, 'Don't be afraid! I have good news for you, which will make everyone happy. This very day in King David's home town a Saviour was born for you. He is Christ the Lord. You will know who he is, because you will find him dressed in baby clothes and lying on a bed of hay.'*

*Suddenly many other angels came down from heaven and joined in praising God... After the angels had left... the shepherds... hurried off and found Mary and Joseph, and they saw the baby lying on a bed of hay. When the shepherds saw Jesus, they told his parents what the angel had said about him. Everyone listened and was surprised. But Mary kept thinking about all this and wondering what it meant.*

### Journey guide

If we ever wonder whether the Christmas story is a fabrication to explain an unplanned pregnancy, the shepherds should convince us otherwise. God invites these unexpected witnesses to be the first people to visit his newborn Son. Unused to being invited to social events, their invitation comes out of the darkness, delivered by angels. Augustus had forced a military peace on their world, but Jesus, the Son of God, brings true peace, uniting people with God and each other.

Coming in from the dark and cold, the excited shepherds must have surprised Mary and Joseph as they came to marvel at the Prince of Peace and explain about their special invitation. Perhaps the shepherds felt a special affinity with Jesus because he too was an outcast, lying in his manger bed in the lowly cattle stall.

### Daily travels

Welcoming those who are outcasts is a strong theme at Christmas. Think and pray about those whom we exclude from our community for reasons of age, creed, race and colour.

### The journey in colour

God's angels surprise the shepherds and show them the way to Jesus. What colours will you use to show the glory of the angels?

---

### Prayer for the journey

 Heavenly Father, make us aware of those whom we exclude from our lives. Give us the compassion to accept others just as they are. Help us to learn from each other and see something of you in everyone we meet. Amen

---

★★★★★★★★★★★★★★★★★★★★★★★★★★★★★★★★★★★★★★★★★★★★★★★★

# A spring in their step

LUKE 2:15–16

The shepherds… hurried off and found Mary and Joseph,
and they saw the baby lying on a bed of hay.

# 27 December

## Walking into a trap

### MATTHEW 2:1–8

 *During this time some wise men from the east came to Jerusalem and said, 'Where is the child born to be king of the Jews? We saw his star in the east and have come to worship him.' When King Herod heard about this, he was worried, and so was everyone else in Jerusalem. Herod brought together the chief priests and the teachers of the Law of Moses and asked them, 'Where will the Messiah be born?' They told him, 'He will be born in Bethlehem, just as the prophet wrote…' Herod secretly called in the wise men and asked them when they had first seen the star. He told them, 'Go to Bethlehem and search carefully for the child. As soon as you find him, let me know. I want to go and worship him too.'*

### Journey guide

The wise men had come to the palace in Jerusalem expecting to find a happy king—a proud father—and his baby son and heir. Instead they found an unpopular tyrant who tried to hide his fear at the news of God's true ruler. Months before this, Mary had predicted that Jesus would drag strong rulers from their thrones and put humble people in places of power. Gripped with a terrible fear of the great power behind the birth of this small baby king, Herod used all his cunning to disguise his evil thoughts. He led the wise men to believe that he wanted only to adore this marvellous child from God. Herod must have thought that he had outwitted God by cunningly using the bearers of the news of Jesus' birth to track down the baby for him as he prepared to follow in their footsteps for the kill.

### Daily travels

Herod reminds us that people can hide behind all kinds of masks. We need to look at people's lives, not just their faces, to tell what they are really like.

### The journey in colour

In our story-map today, we see the wise men arriving at the court of King Herod. From his throne, Herod shows them the scrolls that foretell where the special child will be born. Herod cunningly sends the wise men to track Jesus down so that his soldiers can kill him.

### Prayer for the journey

 Almighty God, we pray for people who live in fear and danger because of those who govern them. We pray for peace and justice for each one of your children. Amen

# 27

# Walking into a trap

MATTHEW 2:7

Herod secretly called in the wise men and asked them
when they had first seen the star.

# 28 December

───────○ 28 ○───────

## Walking alongside

### LUKE 2:22–32 AND 38

 *[Mary and Joseph] took Jesus to the temple in Jerusalem and presented him to the Lord... [Simeon] loved God and was waiting for God to save the people of Israel. God's Spirit came to him and told him that he would not die until he had seen Christ the Lord. When Mary and Joseph brought Jesus to the temple... Simeon took the baby Jesus in his arms and praised God, 'Lord, I am your servant, and now I can die in peace, because you have kept your promise to me. With my own eyes I have seen what you have done to save your people, and foreign nations will also see this. Your mighty power is a light for all nations, and it will bring honour to your people Israel.' ... At that time Anna came in and praised God. She spoke about the child Jesus to everyone who hoped for Jerusalem to be set free.*

## Journey guide

Bethlehem is close to Jerusalem, so this time Mary and Joseph did not have far to travel to bring their baby to the heart of worship—the great temple. Far from home and friends, they may have felt out of place, but God made them welcome. Simeon and Anna immediately recognized this tiny baby to be the Messiah and, as if he was a newly anointed crown prince, they proclaimed to all that Jesus was the long-awaited rescuer. Mary and Joseph must have been amazed at the way God was working out his rescue plan down to the smallest detail.

Simeon and Anna saw with prayerful eyes, unlike the priests who, later in his life, didn't recognize the true identity of Jesus.

## Daily travels

When we pray 'Our Father in heaven...', in time we become more like God, our heavenly parent, in what we do, say and think. After a while, people we don't know can see something of God's likeness, his love, forgiveness and hope in us. What part of your heavenly parent's character would you like others to see in you?

## The journey in colour

Joseph and Mary enter the temple and cross the beautiful tiled floor to give thanks for the safe arrival of Jesus. We see Simeon coming to welcome them. What colours would you use to express your feelings about this encounter in the great temple in Jerusalem?

### Prayer for the journey

 Heavenly Father, sometimes our problems seem so huge that we forget you are bigger than any difficulty. Help us to see your will in our lives. Bring a Simeon or an Anna to encourage us in times of trouble or doubt. Amen

# 28

# Walking alongside

LUKE 2:28

Simeon took the baby Jesus in his arms and praised God...

Reproduced with permission from *Walking with Jesus through Advent and Christmas* published by BRF 2005 (1 84101 360 9) www.barnabasinchurches.org.uk

# 29 December

---
● 29 ●
---

## The hill walkers arrive

### MATTHEW 2:9–12

> *The wise men listened to what the king said and then left. And the star they had seen in the east went on ahead of them until it stopped over the place where the child was. They were thrilled and excited to see the star. When the men went into the house and saw the child with Mary, his mother, they knelt down and worshipped him. They took out their gifts of gold, frankincense, and myrrh and gave them to him. Later they were warned in a dream not to return to Herod, and they went back home by another road.*

### Journey guide

The wise men could easily have missed a small house as they searched for the baby born to be king. Finding a poor couple reduced to living in such lowly conditions, with a small baby, they could easily have gone home in disappointment, their long journey wasted. However, by now the wise men realized that God was doing something extraordinary and they looked with new eyes. All God's signs had been right so far, so, trusting in God, they bowed down to the baby and presented their gifts—gifts fit for a king. Gold, the metal of royalty, was used for crowns and coins. Frankincense was used in temple worship. Myrrh was used at the death of an important person. Gold symbolized Jesus' role as God's true king, frankincense was a sign of his holiness, and myrrh signified the importance of his death.

### Daily travels

Sometimes we miss the extraordinary things of God. Even when they are right under our nose, we still may turn away in disappointment. We need to look with new eyes to see the things of God.

### The journey in colour

Today we see the wise men entering the small house. They are tired from their long journey, but excited to find the newborn king. Bowing down with reverence, they lay their gifts of gold, frankincense and myrrh at Jesus' feet. What colours will you use to show the dark and dirty room, the expensive gifts and splendour of the wise men?

---

### Prayer for the journey

 Lord of heaven, help us not to overlook the signs of your work around us. Show us how to look with godly eyes. Help us not to miss sight of you in the most humble places and to see others as you see them. Amen

---

# 29

# The hill walkers arrive

MATTHEW 2:11

When the [wise] men went into the house and saw the child with Mary,
his mother, they knelt down and worshipped him.

Reproduced with permission from *Walking with Jesus through Advent and Christmas* published by BRF 2005 (1 84101 360 9) www.barnabasinchurches.org.uk

# 30 December

---○─ **30** ─○---

## Walking in fear

### MATTHEW 2:16–18

 *When Herod found out that the wise men from the east had tricked him, he was very angry. He gave orders for his men to kill all the boys who lived in or near Bethlehem and were two years old and younger… So the Lord's promise came true, just as the prophet Jeremiah had said, 'In Ramah a voice was heard crying and weeping loudly. Rachel was mourning for her children, and she refused to be comforted, because they were dead.'*

### Journey guide

Imagine walking out of the cinema 15 minutes before the end of a film. How would we understand the story? Sadly, many people leave the Christmas story too soon and miss the nail-biting climax.

Matthew reminds us that people have two reactions to Jesus—either acceptance (like the wise men) or rejection (like Herod). Herod was angry because, with God's help, the wise men had outwitted his wicked plan to track down the new king. However, he was also frightened of this rival to his power. This is the darkest day in the Christmas story as the destructive force of evil takes control of Herod—a force that is against God's love, mercy and forgiveness. The force of evil enters into the Christmas story, but it is a force that Jesus was born to overcome. The battle will be won at Easter with the victory of resurrection.

### Daily travels

Herod reminds us how one person's fear and anger can draw others into their destructiveness. What destructive forces will you resist today? How will you be a peacemaker in the fight against evil?

### The journey in colour

In his anger, we can imagine Herod tearing the scrolls that helped the wise men to find Jesus, and smashing a cup of red wine. Blood is shed that day in Bethlehem. Herod ordered his soldiers to kill all baby boys aged two years and under in his quest to kill Jesus. What colours will you use to show Herod's evil anger?

### Prayer for the journey

 Lord of all love and lasting peace, forgive us when we feel like hurting others. Turn our thoughts from anger and violence and fill our hearts with the power of your love. Turn us into your peacemakers. Amen

★★★★★★★★★★★★★★★★★★★★★★★★★★★★★★★★★★★★★★★★★★★★★★★★

# Walking in fear

MATTHEW 2:16

When Herod found out that the wise men from the east
had tricked him, he was very angry.

Reproduced with permission from *Walking with Jesus through Advent and Christmas* published by BRF 2005 (1 84101 360 9) www.barnabasinchurches.org.uk

# 31 December

## You'll never walk alone

### MATTHEW 2:13–15

 *After the wise men had gone, an angel from the Lord appeared to Joseph in a dream and said, 'Get up! Hurry and take the child and his mother to Egypt! Stay there until I tell you to return, because Herod is looking for the child and wants to kill him.' That night, Joseph got up and took his wife and the child to Egypt, where they stayed until Herod died. So the Lord's promise came true, just as the prophet had said, 'I called my son out of Egypt.'*

### Journey guide

This time, Joseph's dream was like an alarm bell from heaven. Without hesitation he woke Mary, gathered up the sleeping child, and slipped out into the night—a silent escape on the long road to Egypt. Joseph trusted God and he was not let down: God had even provided the money to live abroad in Egypt—the gold from the wise men.

As Joseph led his small family to safety, he followed in the footsteps of thousands of his ancestors who had been saved by his namesake, Joseph the son of Jacob, who interpreted the Pharaoh's dream and saved his people from death by giving them a safe haven in Egypt.

### Daily travels

It would have been entirely understandable if Joseph had complained to God at this new upheaval. Fortunately, he realized that sometimes our plans need to change and a new direction may be our only real option. Sometimes, it is possible for us to miss God's purpose in our lives because we won't change our plans. Today is a special day to think about new beginnings as we stand on the threshold of a new year with God.

### The journey in colour

On the final step of our journey, the story-map shows Joseph leading his family out of the darkness of danger and into the light of a safe home in Egypt. What colours will you use to express God's hope and safety?

### Prayer for the journey

 Lord of all time and eternity, thank you that you are the God of new beginnings. Thank you that you have a purpose for our lives and that we never walk alone. Help us to see where we might have locked you out of our plans. Help us to listen to your voice and learn to trust you. May we follow you more closely in the year ahead. Amen

# You'll never walk alone

## MATTHEW 2:14–15

That night, Joseph got up and took his wife and the child to Egypt,
where they stayed until Herod died.

# Bibliography

D.A. Carson, *Matthew*, The Expositor's Biblical Commentary, Zondervan, 1984.

Craig A. Evans, *Luke*, New International Biblical Commentary, Paternoster, 1995.

Donald Hagner, *Matthew*, Word Biblical Commentary, Word Books, 1993.

Walter L. Liefeld, *Luke*, The Expositor's Biblical Commentary, Zondervan, 1984.

Robert H. Mounce, *Matthew*, New International Biblical Commentary, Paternoster, 1995.

John Nolland, *Luke*, Word Biblical Commentary, Word Books, 1989.

*Good News Bible* (Maps), Bible Society, 1985.

*Atlas of the Bible* (Maps), Readers Digest, 1983 (out of print).